Mindfulness Made Easy

Martha Langley

D1013658

Teach Yourself®

Mindfulness Made Easy

Martha Langley

First published in Great Britain in 2011 by Hodder Education. An Hachette UK company.

First published in US in 2011 by The McGraw-Hill Companies, Inc.

This edition published in 2015 by John Murray Learning

Copyright © Martha Langley 2011, 2015

The right of Martha Langley to be identified as the Author of the Work has been asserted by her in accordance with the Copyright, Designs and Patents Act 1988.

Database right Hodder & Stoughton (makers)

The *Teach Yourself* name is a registered trademark of Hachette UK.

British Library Cataloguing in Publication Data: a catalogue record for this title is available from the British Library.

Library of Congress Catalog Card Number: on file.

Paperback ISBN 978 1 473 60788 0

eBook ISBN 9781473607897

1

Typeset by Cenveo® Publisher Services.

Printed and bound in Great Britain by CPI Group (UK) Ltd., Croydon, CR0 4YY.

John Murray Learning policy is to use papers that are natural, renewable and recyclable products and made from wood grown in sustainable forests. The logging and manufacturing processes are expected to conform to the environmental regulations of the country of origin.

Hodder & Stoughton Ltd
338 Euston Road
London NW1 3BH
www.hodder.co.uk

Also available in ebook

Contents

Meet the author

I took up meditation in my teens because I thought it was cool. I went to a class and the first instruction was to close our eyes and think of something nice. That was pretty easy. I didn't make it to the next class, but I reckoned I knew how to meditate. If I wanted to cheer up I would close my eyes and think of something nice, and if I wanted to enjoy being sad I wrote poetry. Then something happened – *life*. I was busy and stressed. I gave up being cool, writing poetry and pretending to meditate. It was only years later, after many ups and downs in my life, that I came across the concept of mindfulness, and then I realized that it might have been a good idea to keep on with the classes. Probably, though, I wasn't really ready for it – there isn't much room for 'cool' in meditation practice. Like everyone, I had to come to meditation in my own way and my own time. I hope that your time is now, and that this book will help.

Martha Langley

In memory of Ruth and Keith,
and Reg and Phyll

Preface to the second edition

Mindfulness originated in Buddhism, and as such it's part of a much wider set of beliefs and behaviours. However, in recent years non-Buddhists have become interested in mindfulness and the concept has gradually moved across from the religious context to a more secular one. Of course, some people still embrace the entire Buddhist philosophy of life, but you don't have to do that to benefit from mindfulness.

In fact, you can take on as much or as little as you want or need. For most people, the benefits are directly related to how much effort they put in, but in any case it's entirely up to you what you do.

Mindfulness is a way of learning to live with yourself and with the world you find yourself in. It will help you feel more comfortable and more at ease, and the phrase 'comfortable in your own skin' pretty well sums up what mindfulness is about. Achieving this highly desirable state requires you to undergo a mental journey, learning different ways of being inside your own head, and, come to that, your own body.

This book will focus on the practical ways in which mindfulness can help you. If you find yourself being drawn to deeper issues, you will find plenty of help online and in other books (see Taking it further). There are more spiritual forms of meditation, which tend to require greater discipline from the practitioner, but this book will help you find out whether meditation is for you before you plunge into those more challenging forms.

Much has happened since the first edition of *Mindfulness Made Easy* was published. Mindfulness has become more mainstream, celebrities have written books about it and, generally speaking, mindfulness is seen as the new miracle cure. However, there is still a place for a simple, secular, jargon-free book that makes the central concepts of mindfulness accessible – that's *Mindfulness Made Easy*.

How to use this book

Before you start, get hold of a notepad or open a file on whichever electronic gizmo you prefer, so that you can make notes of your experiences while you're learning about mindfulness. You'll see frequent references to keeping a journal throughout the book, so decide beforehand how you want to do that.

Part one of the book takes you through the various aspects of mindfulness, and some of the more general ways in which it can be helpful. You'll find a series of exercises, which start very gently and which will ease you into the various activities and ways of looking at the world associated with mindfulness. These will probably seem strange at first, so take your time, repeating the exercises a few times each until you feel ready to move on. It's worth reading all of Part one first, as it provides a complete overview. You can choose to either do each exercise before you read on, or read the whole thing before going back and working through the exercises. Don't, however, kid yourself that reading through an exercise is as good as doing it. It isn't.

By the end of Part one you'll have begun to decide whether mindfulness is something you want to pursue. You can't really tell, though, until you've given it several weeks (I suggest eight weeks). During that time you can establish a regular, ideally daily, meditation practice. In Part one you'll also discover that there are other mindfulness tools and you will have explored each one.

Part two looks at more specific ways in which mindfulness can be helpful, from managing stress to improving relationships. You can, as with Part one, read it all or you can read only the chapters that seem especially relevant to you. Throughout, there are exercises and tasks to help you.

Part one

Mindfulness skills

1

Becoming mindful

In this chapter you will learn:

- ▶ *the difference between Being and Doing*
- ▶ *about Doing and your emotions*
- ▶ *about the problems of being on autopilot*
- ▶ *how to become more mindful by noticing what is around you.*

Think back to the last time you had a pleasant surprise – an unexpected gift, a promotion or bonus, or some good news about a health scare. Think about how you felt at that moment. Whether you were relieved, excited, astonished or overwhelmed, you no doubt were entirely caught up in the moment. Seconds before, you might have been feeling tired, or worried about money, or feeling thirsty. All those physical and emotional feelings would have disappeared in the suddenness of the unexpected surprise.

Of course, the moment doesn't last very long. The surprise soon wears off, although you may enjoy the memory for a long time afterwards. Mindfulness encourages you to live every moment with the same intensity and the same letting go of worries and concerns, but without the need for a surprise to make it happen.

Being and Doing

A newborn baby spends its days apparently doing nothing: just Being. Its parents, on the other hand, are quite likely to be in a mad whirlwind of non-stop Doing. They have to work very hard to make it possible for their baby to do nothing but Be. If the parents do get a moment, when all the chores are done and the baby is sleeping peacefully, the chances are they will sit down gratefully and do nothing. Nothing except Be.

Those parents are very aware that their life has gone out of balance since their baby was born – too much to do, not enough time for self – but they also know that it's temporary and soon they'll be able to get back to normal.

However, for most of us, 'normal' is actually quite out of balance – too much Doing and not enough Being. You may wonder why that matters, but it seems that many of the problems people experience arise from that failure to spend time just Being. Stress, for instance, seems to build up when we don't allow time in our lives for Being. Most of us only go into Being mode on holiday, and perhaps not even then. A really busy person will often say that it takes the first week of a holiday to wind down, and only the second week really feels like a holiday.

Perhaps you immediately reacted by thinking that there isn't the time: you have so much to do every day that you can only just manage it; in fact, you never feel quite on top of your workload, and if you took time out for Being – well, nothing would ever get done. There are two answers to this. One is that you have simply taken on too much and may need to re-examine your life and your commitments. The other is that even a short break for time to just Be will send you back to your Doing invigorated and energized, so that you will achieve much more.

Key idea

Mindfulness is a way of redressing the imbalance between Being and Doing.

Try it now: Do nothing

Since you're reading this book, you're already in a situation where there are no other calls on your time, or where you've chosen to ignore those calls for the time that you're reading. So there's no excuse for not doing this exercise. Put the book down and do nothing for two minutes (there's no need to time this exactly). Look out of the window, or close your eyes. Just breathe and Be.

Self-assessment

How did that feel? Think about it for a moment. If you're anything like me, the moment you stopped reading and decided to do nothing, the thoughts started rushing in. Thoughts about the book perhaps, or about what you need to do next, what you're going to eat later on, whether you've got time for all the things you need to do in the next few hours. So even though your body was just Being, your mind was still Doing.

In your journal, record how it felt to do this exercise.

One of the challenges of mindfulness is to gently retrain your mind to accept just Being. If you're still wondering why, think of your mind as like a muscle. It needs to work, and it needs to rest. Even the most dedicated Olympic athletes have rest periods programmed into their training schedule. In fact, these rests are essential, since muscles actually grow slightly larger during rest periods and cleanse themselves of waste products. Your mind is the same; it needs to rest as well as work.

Being and Doing and emotions

There is another good reason for learning to Be as well as Do (or perhaps I should say relearning, since as babies we were all naturally good at Being). Doing mode, which most of us are in most of the time, is not appropriate for dealing with emotions.

Doing mode looks for actions that will produce solutions, but that in turn can lead to knee-jerk reactions, especially to uncomfortable emotions. We react to the pain of the emotion with an overpowering desire to make it stop. For instance, someone who is sad will look for a quick fix to make the sadness go away – chocolate, shopping, alcohol. That may not seem too terrible (although all three can cause problems if taken to extremes), but what about anger? If you feel angry and you make it go away by taking violent action, or doing something else you'll regret later such as walking out of a relationship, then the bad effects of the knee-jerk can be devastating.

Doing mode is all about action and immediate responses. In Doing mode, we look for solutions, set goals and generally try to get on with things. In Being mode, we let go of trying to fix everything and simply look at things as they are. When it comes to dealing with emotions, that space is where you gain a sense of perspective. There will be more about mindfulness and emotions later in the book, but for now let's concentrate on learning to Be.

Try it now: Do even more nothing

Take another two minutes away from reading and do nothing. This time, don't just let your body do nothing: allow yourself to stop thinking too. Thoughts will enter your mind, of course, but when they do, try to leave them alone. Sometimes it helps to think of them as just floating through your mind.

Key idea

I used to have trouble letting thoughts float through, until I was talking about it with a friend. I asked how she did it. 'Well,' she said, 'I don't bother them, and they don't bother me.'

Automatic pilot

There's a funny thing about Doing mode, because even though it's hard to let go of thinking, it's also true that a lot of the time we cruise along busily, not really thinking about what we're actually doing – in other words, we're on autopilot. This is not the same as being in Being mode, because on autopilot we don't really notice anything and we are probably thinking about something else entirely.

Let's say you're taking the short walk from the car park to your place of work. It takes only a few minutes and you've got your head down, perhaps already thinking about the day ahead or maybe talking to a friend on your mobile. In that short walk, you notice nothing about your surroundings. Maybe the tree at the edge of the car park has flowered or lost its leaves if it's autumn, but you don't notice. Maybe someone has dropped a twenty-pound note or left their car unlocked with the keys in the ignition. You don't notice, because you're on automatic pilot.

When you're on autopilot you tend not to notice any of these things. Mindfulness encourages you to stop, switch off the autopilot and really connect with your immediate experience.

Try it now: Being and noticing

Take another two minutes to just Be. Let your mind and your body do nothing, but allow your attention to focus on your surroundings. Whether you were reading on the train or in bed, become aware of the weight of your body against the support, the feel of your clothes against your skin, the air on your face, the light, the temperature, the motion or lack of motion.

Of course, in many ways autopilot is useful. If you're a driver, you probably remember being a learner and struggling to remember all the different skills you had to master to drive a car. Once those skills became automatic, you could focus on the really important business of being a safe driver. You could give your whole attention to the road ahead, the traffic and pedestrians around you, instead of worrying whether you were going to manage your next gear change, or even being distracted by the feel of the steering wheel or the warm air on your face from the ventilation system. The same is true of any skill. We need to practise it until aspects of it become automatic, and then we can move on to the next level.

Autopilot is also very useful when we're in Doing mode. Right now, outside my window, I can see a crab apple tree smothered in blossom. If I kept being distracted by its beauty, I would never get this book written. I'm in Doing mode and that's where I need to be right now.

The problem with autopilot is that you can simply forget to come out of it. It's a question of balance again. When I'm ready for a break from writing, instead of picking up the phone or getting a coffee, maybe I should look at the tree for a moment. A small moment of mindfulness like that is an instant charge-up for my mental batteries.

Because automatic pilot is quite inappropriate for managing emotions, if you forget to switch it off, or it gets stuck in the 'On' position, then that can be disastrous for relationships.

Try it now: A little taste of mindfulness

Eating is one of the things many of us do on automatic pilot. We often eat while barely noticing the food, perhaps because we are in a rush or distracted by the television or radio. This classic mindfulness exercise, devised by Jon Kabatt-Zinn, is normally done with a single raisin, but you can do it with a segment of orange or any small piece of food. You start by picking up the raisin and observing it closely for several minutes. Examine its colour, texture, weight and smell, and see how it reflects the light. Then put the raisin to your lips, and touch it with your tongue – see whether the two sensations are different in any way. Put the raisin in your mouth, but don't chew or swallow it. Instead, feel it in your mouth, against your teeth, cheeks and tongue. When you have fully explored the raisin, then you can chew and swallow it.

Self-assessment

In your journal, record how it felt to do this exercise. Perhaps you felt rather foolish and self-conscious; I certainly did the first time I did it. Nevertheless it is worth doing. Eating a raisin mindfully reminds you that there is a whole world of experience in one tiny piece of food. It is also a good example of what it feels like to come out of autopilot and Doing mode. If you really focus on eating the raisin slowly and with full appreciation then you will stop Doing and stop thinking about all your other concerns. For just a few minutes, you'll have been fully mindful.

Focus points

1 Babies live in Being mode all the time.
2 Adults live in Doing mode much of the time.
3 Adults need to spend time just Being.
4 Being gives your mind a rest period.
5 Doing mode is about taking action and seeing results.
6 Doing mode is not helpful for managing emotions.
7 In Doing mode, we are often on automatic pilot.
8 In autopilot, we are not aware of the present moment.
9 Autopilot is not helpful for managing emotions.
10 Autopilot can get stuck in the 'On' position.

Next step

The next chapter takes you further into the core aspects of mindfulness. You will learn more about becoming fully present in the moment, accepting of whatever is happening and whatever you're feeling, and how to achieve this state of Being without judgement and with kindness to yourself.

2

The core aspects of mindfulness

In this chapter you will learn:

▶ *the value of daily meditation*
▶ *how to live in the moment*
▶ *about acknowledgement and acceptance*
▶ *how to be kind to yourself.*

Mindful living has two components. You can learn to be mindful in your everyday life, and this is helpful in all sorts of ways. You can learn mindful ways of increasing your enjoyment of life and handling difficulties, which can be brought into play at any point in the day. The other component of mindfulness is meditation, which is done in a more formal way, by making a commitment and setting time aside for it. Although meditation has been well known in the West for a long time (it was, for instance, very fashionable in the 1960s), many of us still find the concept a little strange. However, once you start meditating regularly, it soon starts to feel like second nature.

Remember this

Meditation is for everyone. You don't have to wear special clothes, chant or turn into a hippy.

Meditation is the key skill for mindfulness, and it is meditation practice that creates the ability to bring mindfulness into everyday life. Think of a musician practising scales, or all the hours a footballer spends at the training ground. Practice is essential for any skill, and practice is always more than just a rehearsal. The musician acquires mental discipline and focus during practice. The footballer becomes stronger and fitter during training. Both can take what they've acquired into their everyday life.

Meditation is usually done daily, at special times that you set aside for it. However, the great thing about mindfulness is that it encourages you to be extremely tolerant, so if you don't manage to meditate every day you won't need to feel terrible about it or feel like a failure. Of course, as with any new skill, the more you put in the more you will get out. However, if you are only able to put a little in, that's all right. Accept that you'll only get a little out, and that progress will be slow. Slow progress is better than no progress.

Living in the moment

As you already know, mindfulness derives from Buddhist philosophy, and a key component of that is the idea that only the present moment is real; the past exists only in your memory and the future exists only in your imagination. Mindfulness is a way of bringing yourself completely into the present so that you experience it as fully as possible. Like so many of the concepts behind mindfulness, we do already understand it in our culture, but we use a different vocabulary. How about 'quality time'? Doesn't that mean being with whatever is going on (usually we're referring to parenting) 100 per cent, in the moment and totally focused?

You have already had a taste of this in the previous exercises. Other exercises throughout the book will also encourage you to live in the moment.

Of course, the past and the future are still important. Looking back into the past is how we learn from our mistakes, and we need to look into the future in order to make plans. And thinking about both can be a source of great pleasure. But constantly ruminating and dwelling on things that can't be changed (the past) or that may never happen (the future) is an unhealthy habit.

Try it now: Immerse yourself in a mindful object

Stop reading for a moment. Look around you and choose an object to focus on. Spend a few moments looking at it and noting all its qualities. If you can, pick it up and handle it. Notice everything about it – shape, colour, texture, temperature, size, smell and so on. If you can, be non-verbal about this – don't try to give names to the qualities of the object, but instead immerse yourself in whatever it has to offer you.

(If you're reading this in a public place, you may feel inhibited and worry that people will think you're acting strangely. Don't do anything that makes you feel uncomfortable; you can always do this exercise later at home.)

Self-assessment

Record how it felt to do this exercise. Don't describe the object or anything you noticed about it; keep that part of the experience as non-verbal. Just record your reactions.

Acknowledgement and acceptance

When you're being mindful, either during meditation or in your everyday life, you remind yourself how precious the present moment is and how much it's to be savoured. But what about those present moments that are unpleasant, scary or sad? Our natural instinct is to shrink away from pain, whether it's physical or emotional, and yet mindfulness asks you to stay with it and experience it fully. How can that be helpful?

The answer to this question lies in the mindful qualities of acknowledgement and acceptance. Whatever is going on in the present moment, in order to fully experience it you have to acknowledge that it's there. If your mind is thinking about something else, then you aren't really acknowledging it, which is why mindfulness requires focus. But you also aren't acknowledging the moment if you're turning away because something painful or unpleasant is going on.

Let's say that someone is rude to you on the phone – really rude, and it upsets you. Your instant reaction will depend on your character – you might be rude right back, or put the phone down and burst into tears. But then you're quite likely to do something to make the pain go away, to calm yourself down and move on as quickly as possible. This often doesn't work, so that hours later you're still inwardly fuming or tearful about that rude person on the phone.

If you approach this situation mindfully rather than running away from the upset, you'll start by acknowledging that it has happened. Surprisingly enough, doing that can often reduce the intensity of your upset feelings – so that's one way in which mindfulness can help with difficult moments.

The next step is to learn to accept your emotional response for what it is. Emotions can be joyful or painful, but they are always temporary. Instead of climbing right inside your pain and engaging with it, take a step back. Accept that you're hurting, and that it will pass. It's not quite so surprising that doing this means that the painful emotion passes much more quickly, and this is another way that mindfulness helps with difficulties.

Remember this

Whether an emotion is joyful or painful, it is always transitory.

Another word for this process is 'detachment', and this is another concept that can seem a little alien to non-Buddhists. Yet again, we do understand it, but with a different vocabulary. Have you ever been told to count to ten when you feel yourself getting angry? That is just a different way of expressing detachment – in the time it takes you to count to ten, the anger will start to subside and you'll be able to handle the situation more rationally.

Acknowledgement and acceptance are not the same thing as resignation. Resignation implies that there is no hope of change, that you're stuck with whatever-it-is, whereas once you have acknowledged and accepted what is happening for you in the present moment, there is nothing to stop you making changes – in fact, change becomes easier.

Think about how small children experience life. They tend to be totally in the moment, and in that sense they are naturally mindful. On the other hand, they have no ability to detach and observe their emotions as they arise, and are so totally caught up in them that every small problem is, to them, a tragedy. So, in order to be fully mindful, we have to acquire the capacity for detachment as well as the ability to engage with the present moment.

Try it now: Acknowledge and accept

Think back to an unpleasant experience that you had recently. For this exercise, choose something that was mildly distressing. (Later on, when you have confidence in mindfulness, you may choose to explore deeper problems.) Recall the experience and allow yourself to feel the distressing emotions. Acknowledge them, and accept them. Don't try to change anything or rewrite the events in your head.

Self-assessment

In your journal, record your response to this exercise. Later on, after you've had more time to absorb the principles of mindfulness, repeat the exercise and see whether your response has changed.

Being kind to yourself

A big element in mindfully acknowledging something is to be non-judgemental about it. Let's return to the example where someone has been rude to you on the phone. If your instant reaction is to lose your temper and be rude right back, then afterwards you might feel badly about this, or you might spend time righteously justifying your behaviour in order to stop yourself feeling badly. The mindful approach is to accept that this happened. You lost your temper. You can't go back and change it. Now you feel badly about it, accept that too. Don't spend time beating yourself up, but simply acknowledge and accept that you are experiencing a difficult emotion and treat yourself with compassion.

On the other hand, perhaps your reaction was to put the telephone down and burst into tears. Then you feel badly because you didn't stand up for yourself; you let the other person walk all over you. Again, the mindful approach is to acknowledge your reaction, to accept it as something in the past that can't be changed, and to adopt a kindly, non-judging attitude.

Try it now: Be kind to yourself

Go back to the unpleasant experience in the previous exercise. Recall the emotions, which you now acknowledge and accept. If you judged yourself in any way, forgive yourself. Even forgive yourself for being judgemental. The habits of a lifetime can take a while to change.

It's important to be kind to yourself while working on all the exercises in this book. Don't think in terms of success and failure – these aren't relevant concepts. You aren't sitting an exam or trying to reach a certain standard. Each person becomes mindful in their own way and at their own pace, and there's no need to compare yourself with anyone else. Try to feel a sense of warmth and friendliness while you're doing the exercises, and approach each new one with a sense of gentle curiosity. Any difficulties that arise are simply another chance to practise mindfulness.

Try it now: Let go of goals

For this exercise, you need to choose your place carefully, because the idea is to stroll about without any direction and without trying to get somewhere. Don't do it anywhere near traffic, cliff edges or anything else that could be dangerous if you become too absorbed in the exercise. A park, a beach and open countryside are all suitable. Simply start strolling around, with no desire to be anywhere or to achieve anything. Take your time and let your feet carry you where they will, while at the same time being fully engaged in the sights, sounds and smells of your environment. If your mind starts filling up with thoughts, try to let them go. This is not a time for thinking.

Focus points

1 Mindfulness consists of formal meditation and everyday mindful living.
2 Practice is more than just rehearsal.
3 Try to meditate daily.
4 Be kind to yourself if you miss some days.
5 Being mindful means living in the moment.
6 Even negative experiences can be lived fully.
7 Acknowledge and accept whatever is happening.
8 You can detach from your emotions.
9 Be kind to yourself.
10 Learn to let go of goals.

Next step

The next chapter explains the various ways in which mindfulness can help us in many aspects of life and how it can increase happiness.

3

The benefits of mindfulness

In this chapter you will learn:

▶ *how mindfulness can be helpful in many aspects of life*
▶ *how mindfulness increases happiness*
▶ *about the connection between mindfulness and flow.*

In recent years there has been extensive research into the benefits of mindfulness and it is consistently shown to be helpful for both physical health (such as reducing high blood pressure) and mental health (such as reducing anxiety). Of course, we should always keep an open mind about research. For instance, much research involves using university students and they are not a typical cross section of the population, especially since the research looks only at the type of student who volunteers for research. But even with these reservations in mind, it does seem as if learning mindfulness is likely to be beneficial for a wide range of problems. It's also helpful to people who don't have specific problems, but who want to improve their quality of life.

There are various ways in which mindfulness can be helpful, such as:

▶ taking the sting out of negative emotions

▶ taking you away from unhelpful habits of thinking

▶ restoring balance to the two sides of your brain

▶ giving you time out from the increasing sensory overload of the modern world

▶ restoring your natural rhythms

▶ teaching you to live with yourself.

Mindfulness and happiness

What makes you happy? Many people asked this question will pick on special events that made them happy – falling in love, the birth of a child or getting their desired exam results. With this type of event, something happened that brought you entirely into the present moment – you were so happy that you couldn't think about anything else. You lost all sense of yourself and were totally caught up in the moment.

Mindfulness encourages you to engage in the present moment for more of the time, not just when something amazing and special is happening in your life. When you do that, you're more likely to feel happy.

Try it now: Savour a happy time

Think back to the last time you felt totally happy. Take plenty of time to savour the memory.

Self-assessment

Make notes about what you were doing at this happy time, and what was going on in your life.

When people are questioned more closely about happiness, some surprising results emerge. The old adage 'money can't buy you happiness' is only true up to a point. In fact, it can buy quite a lot of happiness if it means meeting your basic needs – enough to eat, a safe place to sleep and so on. After that, people get happier if they can have a little extra – clothes, televisions, holidays. But quite quickly there comes a point where any increase of income, and therefore of material wealth, makes no difference at all to happiness. It also seems to be true that many people become happier as they grow older, perhaps because they are more comfortable in their own skin.

Mindfulness and flow

Although joyful events can bring a great surge of happiness, for many people the happiest time of their lives turns out to be when they were busily engaged doing something that they found totally engrossing. The Hungarian psychologist Mihaly Csikszentmihalyi coined the term 'flow' to describe this experience, although it's also known as being 'in the zone'. He's identified various aspects of flow, all of which need to be present before flow occurs:

► intense involvement with what you're doing

► pleasure in what you're doing that creates a kind of ecstasy

► certainty that you know what you need to do

► feeling competent, and that the task is a challenge but within your abilities

- ▶ no sense of time passing
- ▶ finding reward in the activity itself.

Key idea

The happiest times of our lives are often those when we are totally absorbed in something. My father used to rather touchingly say that the happiest time of his life was when I was small and he was working hard as well as thoroughly enjoying family life. 'Of course,' he used to say, 'I didn't realize it at the time.'

This sense of total engagement is very much what mindfulness is about. It's easy to see that an artist or athlete might have that kind of passionate involvement with what they're doing, but most of us are not that gifted, or we haven't been able to give our whole lives to our passion. Most of us spend most of our time doing the things we need to do (buying necessities, paying bills, cleaning, going to work) in order to make it possible to do the things we really want to do (take holidays, spend time with family and friends, have evenings out, pursue hobbies).

Key idea

Mindful living is a way of engaging with even the dullest task to create flow, rather than waiting for the all-too-few moments when we are free to do what we most want to do. For me, it's easy to find flow when I'm writing or doing research. My big challenge is to bring the same sense of commitment to housework.

Self-assessment

Make a list of those experiences that give you flow. It can be anything that does it for you, even things that other people struggle with (like housework!). Whatever is on your list, they are bound to be activities that you quite naturally and easily become absorbed in.

When you have flow or are 'in the zone', you are doing the things you love doing, and clearly you should try to structure your life, if at all possible, so that you get plenty of opportunities to do them. Nevertheless there will always be other, tedious things that need to be done, and for many of us those activities will take up the majority of our time. If we could generate flow for mundane activities, how much better life would be.

The elements of flow

If you look at your list of things that work for you, you'll probably find that they all have three elements in common:

1 **Rules**
   Some activities have an obvious rule base – paying chess or tennis, for instance. In others, the rules are underlying – for example, I couldn't gain flow through writing unless I had absorbed the rules of language and literacy. Perhaps one reason I don't engage with housework is that I've never taken it seriously enough to learn the rules, and I still don't know whether you're supposed to dust before you vacuum, or vice versa.

2 **Training**
   There is usually an element of skill in activities that create flow, and we acquire skills through training and practice. I always enjoyed reading as a child, but it was only when a new and inspirational teacher started to challenge me that I began to enjoy writing. Skills can be acquired informally, too – I also get flow from gardening, and it's only when I watch a novice struggling to grow things that I realize how much skill I've acquired over the years.

3 **Ritual**
   People nearly always have a ritual, big or small, that eases them into the activity. For instance, a footballer will need to get changed, put on their boots and so on, and most will do this in the same way each time. Some sportspeople are superstitious about the way they get ready, but for others it's simply the way they put themselves into the right mindset. Similarly, when I'm ready to write I like to make a hot drink, sit down, check my emails and then turn to the work in hand.

The three elements in activities that produce flow are also found in mindfulness. There are very few rules in the strict sense, but there are ways of going about mindfulness that need to be adhered to. It certainly takes training, in the sense that you need to meditate regularly before you'll start to acquire the mental skills you need to become mindful. A little ritual that you always repeat before you start to meditate will help you get into the right mindset. You could use a little bell, light an incense stick, or have a special cushion or shawl – whatever works for you.

Other sources of happiness

As well as flow, there are two other commonly identified sources of happiness. Small moments of temporary happiness can come from small things that give you pleasure (a piece of cake does it for me every time). At the other end of the scale, if you feel that your life has a purpose then you're more likely to be happy. Doing something worth while, whether it's in your job, your family or in a volunteering role, will greatly increase your happiness quotient.

Mindfulness increases the intensity of both these types of happiness. If I eat my cake mindfully, I enjoy it far more than if I eat it while reading the paper with the radio on in the background. And anyone who studies mindfulness for long enough will eventually be brought to the realization that everything is interconnected – a concept which brings greater meaning to even small acts of kindness to other people.

Focus points

1 Mindfulness can improve your physical and mental health.
2 Mindfulness can improve your quality of life.
3 Special events make us happy.
4 Having our basic needs met makes us happy.
5 Happiness increases as you grow older.
6 Being totally engaged with something creates happiness through flow.
7 Mindfulness encourages total engagement with all activities, however mundane.
8 Flow requires rules, training and rituals.
9 Small events can also make us happy.
10 A sense of purpose in life creates happiness.

Next step

Before you take the next step towards achieving mindfulness, you need to consider the cautions and concerns set out in the next chapter.

4

Cautions and concerns

In this chapter you will learn:

▶ *how much to meditate*
▶ *about the challenges and difficulties of meditating*
▶ *about the need to have realistic expectations.*

There are a few things to consider before you make a commitment to mindfulness. If you're already working with a therapist, or having help from your doctor for mental health difficulties, then be sure to tell them what you're planning. In the unlikely event that they advise you against starting mindfulness at this time, then leave it for now. You can always come back to it later.

Once you've decided to give mindfulness a try, don't rush things. It's far better to work steadily, reading and absorbing each chapter and taking your time over the exercises, whenever you choose to do them. Mindfulness isn't a quick fix.

How much to do?

Once you start to do regular daily mindfulness practice, don't get caught up in the idea that more is better. If your early experiences of meditation are joyful, you might be tempted to spend more and more time meditating. Or you might be overly enthusiastic at the beginning, thinking that the more you do the more quickly you'll get there.

However, there is no 'there' to get to. In a sense, you're already there, and the job of mindfulness is to help you understand and appreciate that.

To get the full benefit from mindfulness, it is important to make a commitment to regular practice over a number of weeks. Many mindfulness courses run for eight weeks, so that is a good length of time to aim for. By the end of that time you will have found out whether mindfulness is for you, and whether you want to make it a permanent part of your life.

Clearly, you need to find a balance between doing too much and doing too little. If you do too much, you'll struggle to cope with everyday life and perhaps give up early. If you do too little, you won't learn enough about the benefits. It's usually thought that between 30 and 45 minutes is the optimum amount of time to give to a daily meditation session, in addition to small moments of mindfulness throughout the day (you'll find these increase quite naturally as mindfulness becomes more and more part of your life). I suggest that you start with quite a small commitment – perhaps as little as five minutes a day – and build it up slowly but steadily until you reach the right level for you.

(Note: some of the exercises will take longer than five minutes.)

Try it now: Look at your schedule

Examine your schedule and think about your commitments. Ask yourself how you will fit daily meditation into your life.

Self-assessment

In your journal, record your thoughts about how much time you think you realistically have available. We'll consider this further in the next chapter.

It's important to be realistic about what you can manage, and it's far better to meet your commitment than to set the bar too high and then give up. So deciding to set aside five minutes a day, and managing that, will have more benefit than deciding to do 30 minutes twice a day but actually only managing five minutes.

Why some people struggle

There are various reasons why some people find it harder than others to do this kind of work. We've already looked at over-enthusiasm, and overly high expectations can have a similar effect. Being realistic about what you can do and what you are hoping for will greatly increase your chances of success.

Self-assessment

Do you have any worries about mindfulness and meditation? Make a list of them. Examine each one in the light of what you're learning as you read. The information in this chapter should help lay your fears to rest.

TENSION

Meditation is in many ways the opposite of relaxation, but it does encourage release of tension. If you're very tense and wound up, your first few meditation sessions might be quite uncomfortable if that tension should happen to be suddenly released. This doesn't happen to everyone, but it's best to be forewarned. It can feel very odd if you suddenly relax, especially if you've been tense for years, perhaps without realizing it.

Before I started mindful meditation, I tried using a relaxation CD at a very difficult time in my life. It sent me into the deepest sleep I've ever experienced, and waking up from it was very strange. It didn't do me any harm, and it was the first step in a long journey to a calmer life.

Key idea

Everyone should allow themselves time for emerging from meditation. Spend a few minutes sitting quietly while you gradually pick up the reins of your daily life.

Relaxation aims to release physical and mental tension. The simplest exercises concentrate on releasing muscle tension, and many people find that their mind relaxes in parallel with their body. Other types of relaxation exercise aim to create soothing mental pictures (such as a garden, or peaceful beach) – these relax the mind, and often the body follows. In both cases, you enter a quiet and calm mental place where your awareness is lowered, rather like the time just before you fall asleep. In meditation, on the other hand, although you are both quiet and calm, your awareness is heightened.

If you are aware of being very tense, you might like to practise some relaxation before moving on to meditation (some people, however, feel too tense to relax and prefer to start with meditation – see Chapter 24).

Try it now: Do a relaxation exercise

Sit or lie quietly in a comfortable position. Allow your breathing to slow down and become calmer. After a minute or so, scrunch your hands into fists, squeeze them tightly, then open out your fingers and relax your hands. Now work your way round your body, tensing up various muscles, holding them for a moment and then relaxing them. Start at your feet and work your way up. Don't forget the muscles in your face.

Another good way to let go of tension is to have a massage and, again, you might like to try this before moving on to meditation.

TOO SLOW

Some of us only feel comfortable if we're busy all the time and operating at top speed. Some people find even holidays difficult, and no doubt we've all seen the person by the pool or on the beach still busily checking emails on their mobile phone. If you're like that, it can feel like a waste of time to stop, slow down and meditate (or do nothing) for a whole half-hour. It might help if you think of it as time to recharge your batteries, which will help you function far more efficiently when you go back to your normal speed.

FEAR OF CHANGE

Human beings have developed from the Stone Age to the present age by constantly making changes, and yet we all seem to have an inherent fear of change. In fact, it seems from the research that mindfulness practice doesn't change people fundamentally. You'll still be the same person, but you'll function in different, healthier ways.

The various aspects of mindfulness will seem strange at first but, as with anything new, the more you work with them the more familiar they will become. Once you establish a routine and a set of habits around mindfulness, you'll find that you will soon be able to assimilate the practice into your daily life.

TOO SOLITARY

Mindfulness meditation requires you to spend time alone, and yet human beings are naturally gregarious. Our present culture encourages us to be in constant communication with others so that, even if we are on our own, we are often phoning, texting or on a social networking site. If you find it difficult to think of just Being, with yourself and no one else, then remember that you can start with five minutes a day. Just like the busy person, you might find it easier if you think of the quiet time alone as a chance to recharge yourself.

FEAR OF PLEASURE

If you've been unhappy for a long time, you may well have made friends with this state; unhappiness has become your norm and you may be reluctant to try a different way of living. This is a variation on the fear of change, so you should ease yourself in as gently as you like. Remember, kindness to yourself is a core component of mindfulness. Don't, however, decide that mindfulness practice is simply another chore, something that you find hard work, and therefore another reason for being unhappy.

UNREALISTIC EXPECTATIONS

Mindfulness is not about finding a quick answer to all of life's problems; it's much more about learning to accept that life will always have problems. If you go into meditation in the full flood of Doing mode, you'll probably be looking for measurable outcomes and expecting to get the hang of it after one or two sessions. It's quite disconcerting then to find that there is no 'it' to get the hang of. There is no good or bad meditation; there is just meditation. Each session will be different.

Possibly the commonest reason for becoming disheartened and giving up is that most of us find it so difficult to stop thinking. The answer to this is to accept that thoughts will always appear during meditation, and the important thing is your attitude to them. In other words, don't get cross with yourself for having thoughts and don't feel that you've failed in some way. Instead, try not to get involved with the thought; just notice it and let it drift away.

If you do suddenly become aware, in the middle of a meditation session, that your attention has wandered away with the thought and you've been busily engaged in thinking, then bring your awareness back to meditating and let go of the thought. You may have to do this many times in a session, but don't let yourself think of this as a failure. It just happens sometimes. And, each time you lead yourself away from your thoughts, you will learn a little more and you will gently teach your mind to accept that you are going to persevere with meditation.

Try it now: Take just a minute

Sit comfortably where you can see a clock that shows the seconds and allow a minute to pass. While the minute passes, focus totally on your breathing. Don't try to change your breathing or control it; just let it happen – after all, your body breathes quite naturally without any interference from you. This short exercise is good preparation for longer sessions. Repeat it a few times, extending the time you sit for.

If you still have reservations, keep reading. Don't feel you have to start meditating until you are quite ready.

Focus points

1 Tell your doctor or therapist before you start meditation.
2 Be prepared to meditate daily for several weeks.
3 Half an hour to 45 minutes is the usual length of a session.
4 Do less if this is reasonable for you.
5 Start with relaxation if you need to.
6 Accept the need to slow down during meditation.
7 Meditation won't change you fundamentally.
8 Accept that meditation is a solitary activity.
9 Allow yourself to enjoy mindfulness.
10 Have realistic expectations.

Next step

In the next chapter you will find out what resources you will need for mindfulness meditation – both mental and physical – and how to find the best meditation posture for you.

Resources needed for meditation

In this chapter you will learn:

- ► *how to organize yourself for meditation*
- ► *postures for meditation*
- ► *what mental qualities are needed for meditation.*

Formal meditation is the basis on which mindfulness is built, and in order to give yourself the best chance of developing a good practice, there are certain things you'll need to think about first. You will need to consider the best time and place for your meditation practice, as well as paying attention to your posture and how to develop the mental qualities you need.

When to meditate

Since 30 to 45 minutes seems to be the optimum time to spend meditating, you will need to give some serious thought to how you're going to manage this. Many meditators commit to two sessions, at least four hours apart, which means that they meditate for between an hour and an hour and a half each day. One session first thing in the morning and one in the early evening seem to work well, even if the sessions are shorter than the optimum.

Of course, your schedule may make this difficult or even impossible. For many people, weekend routines are quite different from weekdays, and shift workers have even more complicated lives. Only you can work out the best way to approach this. One simple option is to get up an hour earlier than normal and meditate in the peace of the early morning. **Note:** some people find meditation highly energizing. If that turns out to be the case for you, don't do it at bedtime.

Remember this

One session a day, even a very short session, is better than no sessions at all.

Whatever you choose to do, make it regular and realistic and be sure to include enough time to emerge gradually from meditation, so you can sit quietly for a while afterwards. The element of repetition is extremely important – nobody acquires a new skill by just doing it once, and the more times you repeat something the more your brain absorbs and internalizes it.

Research has shown that when we start any new activity it creates new pathways in the brain, and with each repetition the pathways grow stronger. This is known as neuroplasticity, and it's an exciting new development in our understanding of how the brain works.

If you find it difficult to imagine how you'll find the time, think of all the routine things that you do manage to do, from cleaning your teeth to paying your bills. If you place meditation on that list, and make it a non-negotiable part of your life, you'll soon settle into a workable routine. If you worry about spending too long in meditation, and missing something important, such as leaving for work or picking up children, then by all means set a timer. Avoid one with a loud strident ringer, though, and don't sit waiting for it to ring. If you reach the end of the meditation before the timer goes off, that's fine: make the decision to stop and then actually stop.

Self-assessment

You've already looked at your schedule, and begun to decide where meditation might fit in to it. Now consider this in more detail.

Where to meditate

You'll need a quiet place where you can be on your own with no distractions. For many people this means their bedroom, which is fine, but any other private, safe place will be equally as good. (I like to meditate in my bedroom, but I have to make the bed first and put away any bedside reading.)

Turn off your mobile and unplug the landline. Turn off any other electronic equipment in the room, such as a television or computer. Explain to other people that you can't be disturbed during the time you've set aside for meditating. If there are young children around, then make sure that another adult is responsible for them. You can't meditate while listening out for the sounds of trouble.

It can be helpful at first to always meditate in the same place, and carry out the same little rituals of turning things off and arranging the room, as a way of putting yourself into the right mindset. Wherever you choose to meditate, there are bound to be some external noises – distant traffic, a car door slamming, even birds singing. Accepting these and continuing with your meditation is part of the learning process.

Self-assessment

Decide where you will meditate and note in your journal any changes you'd like to make to the location to create a peaceful atmosphere.

If at all possible, add the following to your meditation sessions:

▶ Subdued light in the room – during the day, position yourself with your back to the window.

▶ Comfortable clothing – wear something loose and easy, with no tight belts, cuffs or neck. If possible, take your shoes off.

▶ Be sure to be warm enough.

Key idea

Whatever you're doing, body language is very important. It often tells us more about how someone is really feeling than the words they say. For some reason, we find it easier to lie with our words than with our bodies. It's also true that this can work in reverse – body language reflects how you feel, but if you change your body language you can change how you feel. If you're feeling down, but you stand up a little straighter and try to smile, then you're likely to start feeling a little better. I'm always interested in studying photographs of smiling celebrities on the red carpet – if you look at their hands, they are often clenched, telling quite a different story of underlying tension.

Finding the right posture

The power of body language is why posture is so important when you're meditating – you need to find a posture that supports meditation. Some forms of meditation have strict requirements for posture, such as the full lotus position, which has to be held despite any discomfort. Learning to do this is part of the commitment the meditator makes. However, for the purposes of practical mindfulness meditation, the requirements are less rigorous. (When you're using mindfulness in other ways, during everyday life, no special postures are needed).

You will need to find a posture that is comfortable for you and that you can maintain for the length of the meditation (up to 45 minutes, remember) without too much fidgeting. You can sit or kneel but the main requirement is that you support your own spine – no leaning back against a comfy chair. Meditation is nothing like relaxation, where you look for a position lying down or leaning back fully supported.

The traditional meditation posture is to sit on the floor, in one of the cross-legged positions (not with your legs curled to one side, as this won't allow you to have a straight back). You can cross your legs into a full lotus (where each foot is raised on to the opposite thigh) or a half lotus (where one foot is on the opposite thigh and the other foot is underneath the opposite thigh). Very few of us are supple enough for these postures (I'm certainly not) but there are alternatives.

You can kneel on the floor, with a small hard cushion under your backside, or use a low meditation stool. This puts you into an upright posture without placing your full weight on your calves and feet.

However, for most of us in the West, sitting on a chair will be the most comfortable choice. Choose one that allows you to sit upright, with both feet flat against the floor and with your hips higher than your knees. It might help to slightly raise the back legs of the chair (for instance, with a small pile of magazines). This slightly tilted position makes it easier for you to keep your back straight.

All these positions are balanced, stable and symmetrical and they will help put you in a receptive frame of mind, ready for meditation. You can try various different postures until you find the one that is best for you.

Try it now: Straighten your spine

Try the old trick of imagining that there is a cord attached to the top of your head, which is being pulled gently upwards. This will help you straighten your spine and balance your head.

Meditation postures are often described as dignified, which is how you will look and feel. If dignity isn't quite your thing, then consider the other common description of sitting 'like a mountain'. That's why the lotus and other cross-legged positions are so successful, as they mimic the grounded, solid shape of a mountain, with a broad base tapering to a narrower top. No one will be watching you while you meditate, so forget your normal posture, whether you go for cool, macho or elegant, and aim to be solid and grounded.

Once you've chosen your basic posture, pay some attention to your hands, as these are particularly important in body language. A clenched fist signifies anger, and when we shake hands we share the touch of the more vulnerable palms, signifying trust. So when you meditate, your hands need to be open and relaxed. Most people find it most comfortable to rest their hands on their knees, palms up or down. Palms down will feel like closing the circle, containing you within your own space, whereas palms up is a more open position, receptive to the world around you. You can also rest your forearms on your thighs and allow your fingers to touch. Choose whichever feels appropriate at the time.

Try it now: Find your posture

Experiment with various postures, attempting to hold each one for five minutes. Be sure to straighten your spine and move your head gently from side to side and forwards and backwards until it feels comfortably balanced on top of your spine. Don't try to meditate at this stage; just hold the posture and learn whether it works for you.

POSTURE PROBLEMS

Once you've found the posture that looks likely to be the best one for you, the only problem that's likely to arise is discomfort during a long meditation session. This is not the same as fidgeting, which is a physical habit that should disappear with practice. It's also not the same as restlessness, which is a physical expression of your mental state and which you will inevitably need to deal with during some meditation sessions. (See Chapter 6 for more on this.)

Simple discomfort can arise from holding one position for a long time, especially if you're not used to doing so. Your hips might start to ache, or one foot might go to sleep and start tingling. Some very stringent meditation traditions include tolerating this physical pain to quite extreme limits, but the practical meditation that you are learning doesn't ask that of you.

When you first feel the discomfort, your instinct will be to move, to shift into a more comfortable position, but don't do this straight away. First, try to include the discomfort in your meditation. Allow yourself to feel it mindfully – that is, feel it but don't fight it or judge it. Simply accept it. That in itself may make it tolerable. You may be able to live with it, at least for a while, and in doing so you've made a small step into mindfulness.

As you face your discomfort and accept it, you can also try breathing into it – in other words, as you breathe in, imagine the breath flowing into the part of your body that is uncomfortable. As you do so, allow that part to relax, rather than holding yourself stiffly against the pain. This is a useful technique to practise, and you'll find it cropping up again as you read on.

If you reach the point where you can't tolerate the discomfort for any longer, then make a mindful decision to move. Don't suddenly jerk your knee in a knee-jerk reaction! Decide to move, then quietly and gently move just as much as you need to in order to ease the discomfort. Then settle into your new position and continue meditating.

EYES OPEN OR CLOSED

In the West we seem to instinctively want to close our eyes when meditating. In fact, the usual position is eyes half closed, lids lowered, but not fully. Rest your gaze on a spot a few feet in front of you, and allow your focus to soften so that you aren't really seeing anything. You can choose an object for your gaze to fall on. The preference is for something natural, such as a plant or a wooden object. Choose something with no emotional resonance for you.

If you're more comfortable with your eyes closed, that's fine, but this is more likely to lead to relaxation and even sleep. These are both good, at the appropriate times, but meditation is not about either.

HUNGER AND THIRST

It's best not to meditate immediately after a meal, so leave it about an hour. However, don't meditate when you're hungry, at least at the beginning, because the hunger will distract you. Having said that, some people like to meditate in the early morning before their main breakfast – perhaps a drink and a piece of fruit beforehand is enough to sustain you. Clearly, you don't want to go into meditation thirsty, so have a drink of water or fruit juice before you start. Avoid caffeine, which stimulates, and alcohol, which depresses.

Mental qualities for meditation

We've already seen that the three key qualities of mindfulness are living in the moment, acknowledgement and acceptance, and kindness to yourself. These are the first three in the list of mental qualities needed for mindful meditation. The others are patience, openness, vulnerability, curiosity and concentration.

▶ **In the moment**
While you're meditating you'll focus entirely in the present moment, without any thoughts of the past or the future. Although thoughts will arise in your mind as you meditate, you'll notice them but not engage with them.

▶ **Acknowledgement and acceptance**
The idea is to approach all experience, good, bad and indifferent, in a spirit of calm acceptance. There must be no judging or sense of competition, not even with yourself. This means that there are no 'good' or 'bad' meditation sessions. Each session is as it is.

► **Kindness**
It's surprisingly difficult to learn to be kind to yourself, but it's an essential part of mindfulness. From that you can move on to kindness towards other people. Even small acts of kindness have a profound effect on our sense of well-being.

► **Patience**
You already know that mindfulness isn't a quick fix. It provides a slow, cumulative process of change, so be prepared to be patient.

► **Openness**
Being open to any new experience can be difficult, and mindfulness is no different. Try to clear your mind of any preconceived ideas and allow the experience to unfold as it will. Even slow and cumulative changes can seem scary, but if you come to the experience with an open mind, anything is possible.

► **Vulnerability**
Once you allow yourself to be open to new experiences, you can feel vulnerable, as if your defences are down. You can learn to tolerate this feeling, and with time it diminishes. Take your time and move at your own pace.

► **Curiosity**
Instead of resisting, try being curious about what mindfulness is and the new experiences it will bring you.

► **Concentration**
This can be a tough one. It's one thing to concentrate on a gripping book or when driving in heavy traffic, but meditation asks you to concentrate on almost nothing, just sitting and Being. You'll probably find that you can manage it in short bursts but then your mind wanders and the next thing you know you're thinking about something outside the meditation. As soon as you realize this, stop the thinking and gently bring your attention back to the meditation.

Focus points

1 Decide how to fit meditation into your schedule.
2 Find a quiet private place to meditate.
3 Ease yourself in with a ritual or routine.
4 Posture should be stable and balanced.
5 Do not lean back on a support.
6 Hands should be open, palms up or down.
7 You can learn ways of managing any physical discomfort.
8 Meditation is in the moment, accepting and kind.
9 Allow yourself to be patient, open and vulnerable.
10 Bring curiosity and concentration to meditation.

Next step

The next chapter explains how to try your first short meditation. You will learn how to choose the best time and how to do a breathing meditation.

6

Your first meditation

In this chapter you will learn:

▶ *how to decide when to do your first meditation*

▶ *how to do a breathing meditation*

▶ *about coping with side effects and difficulties*

▶ *how to establish a routine.*

Testing the water

It's time to try your first short meditation. The various exercises so far have eased you in gradually, letting you experience some of the aspects of mindful meditation so that you get comfortable with them. Now you've thought about time, place, posture, mental attitude and so on, you're ready to make a start. First, make a deliberate decision to have your first session on a certain day at a certain time. Don't suddenly decide that you've got a few minutes so you might as well do it. Intention is very important in mindfulness, which means making a decision and sticking to it.

In this meditation you are going to focus on your breathing. It is a simple but powerful meditation and for some people it is the only meditation they ever do. It is also the basic mindfulness meditation.

Try it now: Breathing meditation

When the time comes, retreat to your chosen quiet private space and sit in your chosen position. Take a moment to compose yourself and, if possible, let go of any physical tension. Lower your eyelids, or close them fully, whichever seems comfortable. Bring your awareness to your breathing. Don't change your breathing, or try to control it. As time passes it may become slower and calmer – you can allow this to happen.

Now focus on the sensations associated with breathing. As you breathe in, feel the sensation of the air against the inside of your nostrils, and a slightly different sensation as you breathe out. Just feel it for a few breaths, and then see whether you can feel anything as the breath moves further inside you. Notice whether your chest rises and falls as you breathe, and then whether your stomach also moves gently in and out.

Let yourself be curious about your breathing but not judgemental. Are you breathing fast or slowly? Are your breaths deep or shallow? Does the air feel soft and warm, or is it a little cold and harsh? Now try to take your awareness right into your breathing, feeling it in whatever way works best for you. Let go of any thoughts about your breathing, let go of any words. Hold yourself there, completely absorbed in your own breathing.

After a while, decide to emerge from the meditation. Slowly return to the present time and place. Sit for a while and allow yourself to adjust.

Self-assessment

How was that for you?

In your journal, make notes about your first experience of meditation to help you clarify your response. Do this for your first few sessions, until you've felt your way into meditation.

Breathing meditation debrief

Almost certainly, you will have found your first experience of breathing meditation rather puzzling. It's not the sort of thing that most of us do in the Western world. However, with time it will become more familiar.

You might also have wondered whether you were remembering the explanation correctly or whether you were doing things in the right order. Don't worry; the explanation is there only to give you an idea of what to do. Ultimately, you will bypass the words and go straight to the experience. What I mean by this is that instead of thinking, 'Oh, yes, now I have to notice how my stomach moves when I breathe', you will just do it, in the same way as you can walk without having to think, 'Oh, yes, now I have to bring the back foot forward.' You can bypass both intellect and language and move into direct experience.

It's very likely that you were fine for the first few minutes, remembering what it was that you were trying to do and feeling intrigued and engaged by this new experience. But then came the point when you got to the end of the words from this book, and were just in there, inside your own breathing. Almost certainly you realized, perhaps with a start, that your mind had wandered. You were thinking about work, or money, or Christmas, or any one of a hundred interesting or important things. I hope you remembered to gently bring your attention back to your breathing. If you didn't, don't worry. With enough repetition this will soon become second nature.

To fine-tune your approach to meditation, ask yourself these questions:

▶ Is the place you've chosen working for you?

▶ Was the time right or do you need to change to a different time?

▶ How about the posture?

▶ Did other people respect your request not to be disturbed, or do you need to talk to them again?

Now is the time to put right anything that isn't quite there yet.

Side effects

Sometimes when you clean your teeth you get a twinge from a dodgy tooth. Sometimes when you wash up you have to scrub away at a burnt pan. With any daily activity there will be variations, and some experiences will be better than others. It's the same with meditation. Some days you will have a wonderful time; on others you'll feel less comfortable, or you may feel that it 'just didn't go right'.

The most important thing is that you don't judge or blame yourself in any way. There is no right or wrong; there is only the unique experience that you had in that particular meditation session.

Knowing that probably won't stop you, in the early days at least, from being perturbed if you experience anything unusual or different. To reassure you that there's a huge range of possibilities, all of which are quite normal, here's a list of experiences reported by other meditators:

▶ Feeling very heavy or weightless

▶ Feeling burning hot, or icy cold

▶ Itchy skin

▶ Tingling, numbness, throbbing

▶ Sweating, shivering, trembling, heart pounding, rapid breathing

- Awareness of smells, tastes, sights (especially lights) and sounds

- Feeling disconnected or disoriented

- Odd twinges

- Needing the loo

- Muscle twitches

These sensations stop when the meditation stops, or shortly after, and so if you are very uncomfortable you can always decide to end the meditation and gently bring yourself out of it. If at any time meditation frightens or worries you, don't struggle on with it. Just stop – and talk it through with a doctor, therapist or meditation teacher.

Difficulties

It can be surprisingly difficult to sit and do nothing. Doing mode gets a grip on us and we find all sorts of reasons not to carry on meditating. And sometimes we just can't help falling asleep.

SLEEPINESS

You may be so tired from your busy life that, the minute you stop, you fall asleep. The cure for this is to make sure you get enough sleep at the right time for sleeping. Equally, you may have chosen a time to meditate when you tend to be tired as part of your natural rhythm, in which case try moving the time. The idea that your energy is always low each day at the time of your birth is probably an old wives' tale, but it's certainly true for me that if I meditate at that time I do fall asleep.

On the other hand, the sleepiness may be a trick your mind is playing on you to stop you meditating. Meditation takes you into an alert state of awareness, where your mind is open and you are fully engaged with the moment, whereas when you're asleep you've switched off most of your awareness. This means that, as long as you're getting enough sleep and have chosen a suitable time to meditate, the sleepiness you think you feel is an illusion.

Try it now: How not to fall asleep

Try the following counters to sleepiness:

✳ If your eyes are closed, open them fully, then half-close them for the rest of the meditation.

✳ With your eyes open, breathe deeply a few times to re-energize your mind and body.

✳ Come out of meditation, stand up and move about for a minute or two. Return to meditation – this is a way of signalling to your rebellious mind that you will stick with your decision to meditate.

RESTLESSNESS

This is a simple hangover from Doing mode. Your body wants to keep on keeping on, despite your decision to sit still and meditate. Try taking a little gentle exercise before you meditate, so that your body at least will be ready for a rest. (You could use mindful movement, which is covered in Chapter 8.)

As you become more experienced, you'll be able to detach yourself from your restlessness and watch it without reacting to it. It gives you a good opportunity to practise mindfulness. Notice that you are restless, but then guide your attention gently but firmly back to your breathing.

BOREDOM

Were you told as a child that 'there's no such thing as boredom, only boring people'? It's quite true that, with the right attitude, we can find interest in anything, even paint drying. Mindful meditation could be seen as the ultimate test of this. Just sitting, alone in a room, doing nothing, thinking about nothing, just breathing. How boring is that?

Try it now: Deal with boredom

Here are some tips for dealing with boredom:

✳ Remind yourself of your reasons for meditating.

✳ Remind yourself that your brain, like a muscle, needs to rest.

✳ Accept that you're feeling bored, but decide to continue meditating anyway.

DISTRACTIONS

You already know that, when you set yourself up for meditation, you have to reduce external distractions to a minimum. If any do occur, you can acknowledge them mindfully and continue with your meditation. The same applies to internal, mental distractions, but this can be harder to achieve.

People often find that their biggest difficulty is that in the middle of meditation they suddenly think of something they are sure they will forget if they don't write it down immediately. It is tempting either to come out of meditation to write it down, or to spend the meditation trying to hang on to the thought. However, there are ways of dealing with these mental distractions so that you can continue with your meditation practice. The first thing is to deal with anything immediately pressing before you start to meditate, but remember that most things can wait half an hour.

Try it now: Deal with internal distractions

Here are some tips for dealing with any internal distractions that might occur during your meditation:

* Observe your thoughts mindfully. Acknowledge them, but don't engage with them.
* Accept that thoughts will occur during meditation. This isn't a sign of failure; it's natural. If you find yourself deep in thought, just guide your awareness back to the meditation.

DIFFICULT EMOTIONS

Any one of us is likely to find difficult emotions surfacing during meditation. These emotions may relate to memories from the past or be about something current such as a stressful situation or some problem that is worrying you. Most of us shy away from dealing with this type of thing, and one way of doing this is by keeping busy – by endless Doing. When you revert to Being, it makes a space for difficult emotions to emerge.

First, don't be frightened by what is happening. When you first become aware that something difficult has come up for you, start by simply noticing it. Then, if you feel the need, gently come out of meditation.

Remember this

You can decide to stop meditating at any time during a session, but make this a conscious decision rather than a panicky reaction.

The more powerful the feeling, the more likely you are to engage with it, but as far as possible try only to observe and accept it. Acceptance is the first step on the road to change – you can't change something if you're determined to deny that it's there. This means that ultimately acceptance makes it more likely that you'll be able to move on from the difficulty.

Continue to observe the feelings and stay with them for a while. Also observe where in your body they seem to lodge. This can be anything from tense shoulders to a rumbling gut. If you find a place, try breathing gently and imagining that your breath is moving into that place, soothing and calming it.

Key idea

During meditation you aren't looking for solutions to difficulties or explanations of the past. You're just being with yourself while the difficulties appear. Imagine yourself sitting with a friend who has a problem, and who wants you to hold their hand and be there for them. That's what you're doing for yourself: just being there.

Establishing a routine

Now that you've tried the breathing meditation, you're beginning to get an idea of what it means to incorporate meditation into your life. Try to find the time to sit and do the breathing meditation every day.

It's important to understand that mindfulness is not something you keep in reserve for difficult times. It's impossible to master a new skill if you're under stress or struggling with life for some reason. Although research shows that mindful meditation can help with some chronic problems, such as depression, stress and high blood pressure, it doesn't make sense to wait until these things strike before you consider it. In any case, the benefits to be had from meditation are consistent, regardless of how well or badly your life is going.

Once you've decided on a regular meditation routine, do try to stick to it. Keeping your promises to yourself is an important part of mindfulness, which is why it's also important to set up a routine that is practical and within the bounds of possibility for you, given the specifics of your life.

If you find that you aren't able to maintain the routine, don't beat yourself up about it. If you miss a few sessions, you'll find that when you start again you'll realize how much benefit you were getting when you did meditate. You'll have learned something, and that's always valuable.

Focus points

1 Intention is important.
2 Focus on your breathing, but don't try to change it.
3 Feel all the sensations associated with breathing.
4 If your mind wanders, gently bring it back.
5 Take time to emerge from meditation.
6 There are occasional side effects.
7 You may feel sleepy, restless or bored.
8 In time, you will learn to ignore distractions.
9 Sometimes emotions emerge during meditation.
10 Work out a daily routine for meditating.

Next step

The next chapter explains a mindfulness exercise that aims to improve well-being by supporting and exploring the mind–body relationship. Called the body scan, this exercise focuses on paying attention to your body in a structured way so that you increase your awareness of every part of it and at the same time release tension.

7

Doing a body scan

In this chapter you will learn:

► *about the importance of the mind–body relationship*

► *how to increase body awareness by doing a body scan*

► *how to release physical tensions arising from an emotional source.*

We've already looked at how body language and mood are closely interrelated. That's all part of a bigger picture of mind–body interactions, which we do tend to ignore although the proof is all around us. It can be hard, for instance, to accept that a physical pain can feel greater or less according to our state of mind, and yet most people have had the experience of feeling unwell but forgetting all about it when something good happens. Sporty people all know that they don't usually feel the full pain of injuries until they're back in the changing room. If you're fully engrossed in sport and enjoying yourself, your mind doesn't notice the pain.

We express our emotions physically, with both facial expressions and body language. Someone who's happy tends to be physically animated; a sad person tends to be inactive. If there is a sudden joyful event, we tend to jump around and hug one another, whereas overwhelming grief might make us throw ourselves to the ground and howl.

There are other, less obvious ways in which mind and body are linked. You've probably experienced butterflies in your tummy when you're nervous, or experienced worry as if it were a great weight in your chest. And sometimes you are still carrying the physical effects of emotions relating to events far in the past.

Self-assessment

Where in your body do you feel the following emotions: excitement, sadness, worry and happiness? Note them down in your journal.

A part of mindfulness is to become more aware of your body, so that you reinforce the mind–body connection and understand how this works for you as an individual. Nurturing that connection is part of a holistic (or 'whole person') approach to your well-being.

Body scan explained

Body scan is a mindfulness exercise that aims to support and explore the mind–body relationship. It focuses on paying attention to your body in a structured way on a regular basis.

As with the breathing meditation, you should read the following description of the exercise carefully, but eventually, after enough repetitions, you won't need the words to guide you; you'll simply know what to do.

It's usual to do this exercise lying down but you can do it sitting in a comfortable chair. You should be somewhere warm and quiet where you won't be disturbed. Loosen any tight clothing and kick off your shoes if possible. As with meditation, turn off anything that might distract you, such as a phone, and explain to other people that you don't want to be disturbed. Set a timer if you need to be aware of the time (allow half an hour for the exercise). Although you normally do body scan lying down, it's not a relaxation technique, and if you find you feel sleepy or overly relaxed, then try it the next time sitting instead.

Try it now: Do a body scan

Start by breathing mindfully for a few minutes to put yourself into a clear mental space. Let go of all your daily concerns and allow yourself to settle into the exercise.

As you breathe, allow yourself to connect with your body. Notice how it feels, the weight of it supported by the chair or bed. Notice any general discomforts, aches and pains.

Then take your awareness right down into your left big toe. Do this by breathing in and mentally travelling down your left leg until you reach the toe. Feel as if your awareness is travelling down the leg as you take in the breath. When you breathe out, imagine the breath leaving your toe but leave your awareness in the toe. This may seem a little strange at first, but work with it until you find a way that feels right for you – the aim is to be connected with both your breathing and different parts of your body.

Once your awareness is established in your left big toe, take a moment to feel any sensations in it. Feel whether it is comfortable, tingling or aching. Feel the clothes that are touching it, or maybe the touch of the next toe along that is leaning against it. Don't judge anything – for instance, some big toes are quite bent, heading for a bunion or maybe already there. Don't start thinking about how it's your own fault for wearing the wrong shoes.

The aim now is to take your awareness to each part of your body in turn, following the order given below. As you do so, feel the physical sensations, both internal (e.g. warmth, aches) and external (e.g. clothes). Also allow yourself to feel any mental or emotional sensations that arise. Although feet are extraordinarily sensitive, it is more common to find mental and emotional sensations in the abdominal area – stomach, chest and shoulders particularly.

Here is the order for doing a body scan:

1 Breathe down into your left big toe, feel each of the toes in turn, the sole of your foot, coming round to the heel and ankle. Take your awareness up through the calf and then into your knee, followed by your thigh. Take your awareness across your pelvis and breathe down into your right big toe. Repeat the procedure given for the left leg, working your way gradually back up the right leg.

2 Next, take your awareness into your pelvis, hips, buttocks and genitals. (Try to treat this sensitive area in exactly the same way as the rest of your body.)

3 Bring your awareness into your lower abdomen. Now you can feel your stomach moving gently in and out with each breath, as well as being aware of any internal sensations. Take a little longer to feel any emotions that may arise.

4 Move up to your ribcage, which also moves gently as you breathe. Continue to be aware of internal, external and emotional sensations.

5 Take your awareness to your chest and throat. When you reach your face, take your awareness into the muscles of your face as well as your jaw, eyes, nose and mouth. Move up into your skull, over the top of your head, and then down into your neck and shoulders. From your shoulders, breathe down into your left thumb, feel each finger in turn and come back up your arm feeling the muscles, the elbow and the shoulder. Repeat in the same way with your right arm.

6 When you return to your right shoulder, move your awareness slowly down your spine until you reach the small of your back. From there you can expand your awareness slowly to embrace your whole body. Let your breath move outwards into every area and feel as if your mind and body are breathing as one.

7 Open your eyes and gently re-emerge into the world.

Body scan debrief

For quite a long time I found it difficult to breathe into the different parts of my body, and I felt that my awareness travelled more easily on the out-breath. I didn't worry about this, and gradually I changed my mental approach so that my awareness moved on the in-breath.

The body scan often produces a feeling of peace and well-being that lasts for several hours afterwards. If this doesn't happen for you, don't feel you've failed. It's still important to do a body scan in order to strengthen your mind's connection with your body. You may even at times feel quite upset, or reluctant to carry on. Do as much as you feel able to do each time, but do persevere with repetitions as it is a valuable exercise.

One way in which body scan is beneficial is that it helps bridge the gap between Doing mode, where most of us are so comfortable, and Being mode, where most of us are still learning to be comfortable. While your attention is on your body you are fully focused, and yet you are Being rather than Doing. Do be careful not to get dragged by your mind into thinking about your body in a Doing way ('I must lose that last bit of belly fat,' 'I wish I had better muscle tone,' 'I wonder why my knee aches' and so on).

Remember this

Throughout the body scan, allow yourself to feel each part of your body without judging.

EMOTIONAL RELEASE

Although you may become aware of emotions during a body scan, it's unusual for these to feel so strong that you can't cope. If this should happen to you, though, stop, and arrange to talk to a doctor or therapist about it. It's more likely that you'll experience any emotional release gradually, in easy stages. If this happens, observe it mindfully but don't engage with the emotions. In time and with repetition, you'll learn more about how your body expresses emotions, and you'll be able to let go of some of your physical tensions that have an emotional source.

Focus points

1 Body language and mood are closely related.
2 We express our emotions physically.
3 The body scan strengthens the bond between mind and body.
4 There is no special posture for a body scan.
5 As you breathe, take your awareness into various parts of your body.
6 Take time over parts where you carry your tension.
7 Take time over parts where you feel your emotions.
8 Don't be judgemental about your body.
9 Be prepared for emotional release.
10 Allow yourself to stop if the emotions are too powerful.

Next step

In the next chapter we explore how mindful movement – stretching and walking – helps us prepare mentally for meditation.

8

Mindful
movement

In this chapter you will learn:

▶ *how mindful movement and stretching are a way of preparing mentally for meditation*

▶ *different ways of stretching mindfully*

▶ *formal and informal approaches to mindful walking.*

Body scan helps you strengthen your mind–body connection. Mindful movement takes this a stage further. You can use mindful movement, especially mindful stretching, as a way of easing yourself into the right mental place for a meditation session. You'll also find it helpful when you start to practise mindfulness in your daily life – it can act as a bridge between meditation and mindful attitudes in everyday situations. While you're engaged in mindful movement, stay in tune with your breathing. If your mind wanders, gently bring it back to focusing on the movement.

Anyone who has a physical disability can still practise mindful movement, as it's only ever necessary to work within your own physical limits. There are no goals or absolute standards, only you with your body and what you can manage.

Try it now: Do a mindful movement exercise

Stop reading and sit quietly for a moment. Take your awareness to your breathing and let yourself settle quietly. Close your eyes. Decide which hand you will use for the exercise, and gently open the fingers. Now move the fingers as slowly as you can until your hand is closed in a fist. Feel how your hand carries out this action, how the fingers gradually come together and how the thumb folds itself inside the fist. If you can't close your hand fully, perhaps because of arthritis, do as much as you can.

Mindful stretching

Don't think that stretching is only for sporty people as part of their warm-up. Everybody knows that athletes stretch to warm up before an event, but it's less well understood that we can all benefit from regularly stretching out our muscles. It is actually very energizing. If you are feeling tired but still have more things to do, a few minutes of mindful stretching will give you an energy boost.

Some of the documented benefits of this are:

► greater flexibility of muscles and joints

► better posture

► improved blood circulation

► better co-ordination

► stress relief and relaxation

► higher energy levels

► increased sense of well-being

► pain relief.

Mindful stretching consists of slowly stretching various parts of your body until you reach the limit of what is comfortable for you (known as 'the edge'), and then exploring what this feels like. Remember to be aware of your breathing as you move.

Try it now: Do a mindful stretching exercise

From a sitting position, slowly stretch upwards with both your arms. Go right to the edge of your personal comfort zone, reaching upwards. Then move your arms slowly out and down until they are resting by your sides, keeping them as fully stretched as possible.

Self-assessment

How did that feel? You can learn a lot from your mental reactions to being on the edge of a stretch. (Repeat the exercise if you weren't following your mental reactions the first time.) Keep a record in your journal of your experiences during mindful stretching.

What have you learned about yourself? Are you the kind of person who tends to power through any discomfort, or do you hold back, reluctant to feel where the edge is in case it hurts? In the first case you're more likely to injure yourself during physical activities, in the second you'll find it hard to improve your physical skills. There is a happy medium, which consists of learning to tolerate the discomfort of being on the edge, without pushing your body further than it's ready for.

Understanding your attitude is important for two reasons:

▶ You're learning to be more sensitive to your own body and more in tune with it.

▶ You can use this knowledge to examine how you react to emotional pain.

Do you treat emotional pain in the same way as physical pain, either ignoring it and pressing on regardless, or shying away and never feeling able to face it? Or are you the opposite, pushing yourself too far with one type of pain but shying away from the other type?

There is another lesson to be learned from mindful stretching. When you reach the limit of the stretch and try to hold it, you'll become aware of the fact that your body is never entirely still. You'll notice this especially if you do stretches while standing up, where, in order to keep your balance, your body will constantly make small adjustments to your position. The same is true of life. In order to lead a balanced life, we need to make constant small adjustments.

You can do any type of stretching in a mindful way. Here are a few suggestions for stretches that you can do while sitting, standing, lying down or on all fours.

SITTING STRETCHES

1 Stretch your arms up till you reach your limit, and then bend from the waist, first to one side then to the other.

2 Lift your feet up until your legs are straight, then point your toes.

3 Stretch your arms up till you reach your limit, then bend forward to try and touch your toes.

STANDING STRETCHES

1 Take a step forward with your right foot, allowing the left leg to stretch out behind you. Repeat by taking a step forward with your left foot.

2 Stretch your arms up till you reach your limit, and then bend from the waist, first to one side then to the other.

3 Stretch your arms out on either side at shoulder height. Twist from the waist, first to one side then the other.

4 Stretch your arms up till you reach your limit, then bend back slightly and then forward to try and touch your toes.

LYING DOWN

▶ Lift one leg as high as you can. Lower it, then repeat with the other leg.

ON ALL FOURS

▶ First arch your back with your neck bent forward and head between your arms, and then relax and raise your head and make your back curve downwards.

Key idea

If you find mindful stretching beneficial, consider taking up yoga, which can be developed into a form of meditation.

Mindful walking

Walking is one of the great autopilot activities. Indeed, many people say they do their best thinking on a walk, once they've settled into a steady walking rhythm. However, it is well worth walking mindfully on occasion. This will reground you and put you back in touch with both your body and your environment. This exercise is where you begin to cross the bridge from mindfulness practice to mindfulness in your daily life.

You can use mindful walking at any time, and many people find it helps them arrive at their destination with a calm, clear mind.

Remember this

It is best to do mindful walking on your own. If you have a companion, it will be difficult to resist the urge to talk.

Try it now: Informal mindful walking

You can choose to do this if you are walking to a specific place, or if you're walking for the sake of having a walk, but it's best if you're walking somewhere familiar where you don't have to check a map or follow directions. Start with a short walk of a few minutes, not more than half an hour maximum. The only thing you should carry is a rucksack, as anything else will leave you unbalanced. Turn off your phone and make a firm resolution not to mull over problems, make plans or do any of the sort of thinking that normally takes over when we're walking.

Set out on your walk and focus your awareness on your breathing as you walk. Then take your awareness into your body, and feel how all the parts work together to enable you to walk. In fact, you can turn this into a walking body scan if you choose. Once you've become fully aware of your own body, move your awareness outwards. Pay attention to your environment, feel the air on your face and see whatever there is to be seen, hear the sounds and smell the smells.

Self-assessment

How did that feel? In your journal, record the sensations you experienced during your mindful walk.

Mindful walking as meditation

Formal Buddhist practice includes an extreme form of mindful walking which is used as an alternative to sitting meditation. For most of us this is stranger and more difficult than informal mindful walking. To do it, you need a private place where you can take a few steps in a straight line – say between five and ten. It's good to do this in the open air but, unless you're on a retreat (see Chapter 13), you'll probably prefer to be sure that nobody can see you, so choose your place carefully.

Try it now: A mindful walking meditation

By all means do this exercise barefoot if it's safe to do so.

1 Stand quietly for a moment with your arms by your sides and settle into awareness of your breathing. Become aware of your contact with the ground.
2 Lift the heel of one foot very slowly and bring it forward in a step. Do this as slowly as you can, make the movements barely perceptible.
3 When that foot is on the ground, lift the heel of the back foot as slowly as you can and take another step.
4 Try to be aware of every sensation in every part of your body as you take a series of infinitely slow steps.
5 At the end of your space, turn slowly and stand for a moment before returning the way you came.

Self-assessment

How did that feel? In your journal, record your sensations during the mindful walking meditation.

Your first attempt at a mindful walking meditation probably felt very strange. It's quite alien to most people at first, and yet it continues the important process of putting you fully in touch with your body. This is a difficult form of moving meditation, and while you're getting used to it you can devise a form of words that help to keep you focused. Use whatever works for you, but aim for a series of mental notes that describe the stages of each step, such as 'heel up, arch stretched, move on to ball, push off with toes, lift foot' and so on. After a few repetitions, you won't need the words and you can experience pure, slow mindful walking.

Remember this

While doing the mindful walking meditation, stay in tune with your breathing, and keep the movements small and slow.

Focus points

1 Mindful movement helps you bring mindfulness into your everyday life.
2 Mindful stretching can be a preparation for meditation.
3 Stretching is good for your muscles.
4 Always be aware of your breathing as you stretch.
5 Stretch to your limit but not beyond.
6 Your body is never completely still.
7 Stretching will teach you about your own reactions to pain.
8 Mindful walking meditation is super-slow.
9 Informal mindful walking takes you off autopilot.
10 Informal mindful walking helps clear your mind.

Next step

The next chapter explains some other forms of meditation: meditation with focus, meditating around a topic, guided meditation and loving-kindness meditation.

9

Other meditations

In this chapter you will learn:

- ► *how to meditate with focus*
- ► *how to meditate around a topic*
- ► *how to do a guided meditation*
- ► *how to do a loving-kindness meditation*
- ► *how to deal with difficulties in your loving-kindness meditation practice.*

Many different meditation disciplines have developed from different parts of Eastern culture, and each one can be a lifetime's study. However, meditation can also offer great benefits to someone who incorporates it into an existing lifestyle. Once you've begun to meditate, you may find your practice changing as your needs change. Although the stricter meditation disciplines wouldn't allow this, within the looser approach of Westernized mindfulness it's perfectly acceptable.

Meditation with focus

In the breathing meditation discussed in Chapter 6, your focus is on your breathing and you gently bring your mind back to your breathing if it wanders. However, you can also focus on other things, such as:

▶ a candle flame (don't set the candle too close)

▶ a natural object such as a pebble

▶ a prayer or religious image

▶ a chant, a mantra or an affirmation.

As with a breathing meditation, you use the same technique of settling yourself physically and mentally before focusing on the item you've chosen. If your mind wanders, again, don't beat yourself up about it; gently bring it back. If thoughts appear, just let them be.

This kind of meditation can bring feelings of great calmness and tranquillity, although of course these are likely to wear off between sessions when you return to your normal life.

Try it now: Meditate on an object

Choose an object – the candle, a natural object or a religious image – and set it in front of you while you meditate. Start your session with mindful breathing to settle yourself, but then move your awareness to the object.

MANTRAS AND AFFIRMATIONS

In traditional practice, your mantra is given to you by your meditation teacher. It is chosen for you personally and you are cautioned never to reveal it. It usually consists of one or two meaningless syllables, and the idea is to repeat the mantra to yourself in a rhythmic, unemotional way with each out-breath. This becomes a type of chanting.

It is possible to choose your own mantra. You can choose either a meaningless syllable or a simple word that has a positive resonance for you (although, in practice, it can be hard to find a word that is entirely positive). The simplest mantra is 'Aaaah', the kind of sound you make when you finally sit down after a long, hard day (not the sound you make when pleasantly surprised).

Affirmations are different in that they have meaning. They can be very powerful ways of changing how you see yourself and how you feel about yourself. You can repeat the affirmation aloud or say it in your head. You can also change your affirmation as your needs change; some people find that they will use several different affirmations over time.

Here are a few simple rules for creating affirmations:

▶ Keep it short.

▶ Use 'I'. Say 'I love life' not 'Life is good'.

▶ Use the present tense. Say 'I am happy' not 'I will be happy'.

▶ Use positive statements. Say 'I feel well' not 'I don't feel ill'.

Key idea

It is possible to choose both your own mantra and an affirmation. Once you have decided on them, make a note of them in your journal.

Try it now: Meditate on a mantra or affirmation

Repeat the exercise above, this time using your chosen mantra or affirmation as your focus.

Meditation on a topic

Once meditation is well established as a habit, you can try meditating on a specific topic. Start with something that is entirely positive for you. Later, you can meditate on something that's troubling you. This is not the same as thinking it through, problem solving or goal setting. On the contrary, you simply allow yourself to explore the topic without expecting to arrive at answers or judgements. To return to our earlier example of someone being rude to you on the phone (see Chapter 2), you could meditate about that experience. However, you would *not* expect to:

► work out what you could have done differently

► work out what was going on for the person who was rude

► soothe yourself if upset (although the meditation itself might have that effect)

► convince yourself that in the overall scheme of things the event wasn't that significant.

 Try it now: Meditate on a topic

Choose a topic for meditation. Start with something positive for you before going on to more troubling topics. Start with mindful breathing, and then bring your attention to the topic. Stay with it, and remember not to judge.

Guided meditation

Guided meditation means simply that a voice – recorded or real – takes you through a meditation. It can be on something fairly straightforward, such as relaxation, or it can be around a topic of deep significance, such as the power of love or the nature of reality. Guided meditations often include a strong element of visual imagery. You can listen to guided meditations on a CD or MP3 player, watch a video or attend a class.

Meditation with no focus

The most demanding forms of meditation are probably those with no specific focus and pure mindfulness, as practised in the Buddhist tradition. This doesn't mean that you have to meditate in this way, because, as you know, mindfulness has changed as it has become assimilated into Western culture.

It can take many years to make progress with this type of meditation. It is underpinned by the Buddhist belief that we are all, whether we are happy or sad, living inside an illusion. Our reality is not real at all, but something we create to get through life. This type of meditation aims to concentrate entirely on the moment and the nature of reality and it has the ultimate aim of demolishing the illusion.

You might ask why anyone should put so much effort into this, and the answer is that, once the illusion is destroyed, which can take years, the meditator is liberated into a whole new experience of reality. This liberation is permanent, whereas with other types of meditation the effects wear off between sessions.

Loving-kindness meditation

It's too late now to change the name we use for mindfulness, but it is slightly misleading. For a start, it isn't really about your mind. And also, the English word 'mindfulness' doesn't really capture the full meaning of the original word. It's been suggested by some that 'heartfulness' would be a more accurate translation. Whatever we choose to call it (and Buddhists call this type of meditation *metta*), mindfulness includes a strong element of kindness – to yourself, to others and, ultimately, to the entire universe. However, it starts with kindness to yourself.

Key idea

Loving-kindness meditation is best undertaken after you've explored simpler forms of meditation for a while.

Try it now: Loving-kindness meditation 1

You can carry out this meditation in any position, sitting or lying, but it's important to be comfortable. Start, as usual, by focusing on your breathing to settle yourself into Being mode. Now bring your awareness to yourself and let go of any judgements or negative thoughts about yourself.

Try wishing yourself well: 'May I be happy, healthy and safe.' If you find this hard, try using your own name: 'Martha, may you be happy, healthy and safe.'

If you prefer to visualize, then imagine yourself as a tiny helpless baby. Imagine that you're holding the baby in your arms and creating warmth and security for it.

Self-assessment

How did that feel? Many of us find it quite difficult to do this, and yet we need to learn to be kind to ourselves before we can extend kindness to other people. Record your experience of loving-kindness to yourself in your journal.

Try it now: Loving-kindness meditation 2

Repeat the first exercise but, after focusing on yourself, move on to thinking about another person, someone you care about. Bring them to mind and wish them well in the same way as you did for yourself. Then move on to another person that you know in a neutral way – an acquaintance. Wish them well. Next think about someone you aren't so keen on, perhaps someone you don't get on with at all. Wish them well.

You will find that you have enough kindness in your heart for all four people (remember, you need to include yourself). Indeed, you'll be able to keep extending the boundaries as you repeat this meditation until you encompass the entire universe.

DEALING WITH DIFFICULTIES

By the time you have tried all the different meditations in this chapter, you'll have practised dealing with difficulties such as your mind wandering or thoughts and emotions intruding. Of course, they'll still be there, as they never entirely go away, but you should be feeling more confident and less anxious when this does happen.

When you try loving-kindness meditation, you may find other difficulties arising.

▶ Feeling nothing

You might find it difficult to conjure up kindly feelings, or to think of a suitable person for one of the categories, or indeed anyone at all. Just work with whatever you've got each time.

▶ Feeling too much

It's quite common to feel emotions welling up as you do this meditation. Try to carry on, but don't push yourself too hard. You can do this meditation in small stages, thinking of one category of person at a time. If it all gets too much for you, allow yourself to stop and quietly return to normal awareness. Take a moment to feel the emotions, and let them subside naturally.

▶ What 's the point?

You might find yourself resisting the entire notion of practising loving-kindness. Perhaps you think you already know who you care about and who you don't, and that's fine with you. The point, though, is that the meditation helps you let go of negative feelings such as anger and jealousy. As long as those are festering inside you, you'll struggle to be fully mindful.

▶ Aren't there better ways?

If you're very locked into Doing mode, you might well think that your time would be better spent doing good rather than thinking kindly. The answer to this is that you will be a much more effective doer of good if you're in tune with yourself, and acting from motives of pure loving-kindness.

Focus points

1 You can meditate with focus.
2 A mantra is meaningless and is repeated rhythmically.
3 Affirmations have meaning.
4 Affirmations should be short, positive and in the present tense.
5 Meditation on a topic is not solution oriented.
6 Guided meditation involves listening to a voice.
7 With most forms of meditation, the effects wear off.
8 Pure mindfulness meditation will break the illusion of reality.
9 Breaking the illusion of reality is a permanent effect.
10 Loving-kindness meditation can be extended infinitely.

Next step

The next chapter will show you how to begin to incorporate mindfulness into your daily life.

10

Mindfulness in everyday life – the basics

In this chapter you will learn:

▶ *what is needed for everyday mindfulness*
▶ *how to bring mindfulness into your everyday life*
▶ *some mindful activities.*

Mindfulness is grounded in meditation, and the experience of regular meditation will gradually feed into your everyday life. However, you can also make deliberate efforts to incorporate mindfulness into all aspects of your life. This will be a highly individual process, since each of us has different routines and different needs.

It's really important to understand that it is only your practice of meditation that makes everyday mindfulness possible. Without regular meditation you will have no foundation for living a mindful life.

Remember this

Regular meditation practice is the foundation of everything. When you call on mindfulness skills in the turmoil of normal life, it will only be the fact that you've practised at special times set aside for meditation and nothing else that will make this possible. As an analogy, my partner likes to go kayaking in dangerous places, at sea and on wild rivers. He is able to stay safe in dangerous waters because of the many hours he spends practising his skills on the safe, calm water of our local lake.

What you need

To achieve everyday mindfulness, you need the same physical and mental resources that you need for meditation practice.

TAKING THE TIME

The more time you are able to spend being mindful, the more benefits you'll feel. When you first start, it may feel as if some activities take longer than they used to, but soon you'll realize that giving your whole attention to something is not only more rewarding but almost always more efficient. You will need to set a little time aside for specific mindfulness exercises, but you'll also find that some activities can be done mindfully without setting time aside especially.

Wherever you are, whatever you're doing, you can choose to do it mindfully. Since I am – eventually – going to have to dust anyway, it won't take any more time for me to do it mindfully.

CHECKING YOUR POSTURE

There are no special postures for being mindful in daily life, and the task you're engaged in may well dictate how your body needs to behave. However, we've already seen how important body language is and how changing your body language can change your mood. So before you start a mindful activity, check your body language.

▶ If you're sitting, sit up straight rather than slumped or sprawled.

▶ If you're standing, stand straight with your head well balanced on your shoulders.

▶ Make your movements purposeful.

MENTAL RESOURCES

The mental resources needed are much the same as for meditation, although you may find it more of a challenge to incorporate them into daily activities. There are plenty of opportunities to be mindful, but remembering this isn't always easy in the hustle and bustle of normal life.

▶ Living in the moment

This can be tough when you're doing something that is rather tedious such as queuing at the supermarket checkout, but it can be done.

▶ Acknowledgement and acceptance

How many times a day are we given the chance to practise acceptance? It can be anything from accepting that the queue is moving slowly to acknowledging that your boss is upset with you and nothing you can do will change that.

▶ Kindness

We all have endless opportunities every day to be kind, both to ourselves and to others. It's often just a case of coming out of autopilot and remembering to do it.

▶ Patience

In this context, patience is about accepting that it will take time to incorporate mindfulness into your daily life. You'll probably find that at first whole days go by without you remembering to be mindful, but gradually the effect of regular mindful meditation will bring you more and more in tune with mindful living. In the transition period, choosing to do specific things mindfully during the day will help you establish the habit.

▶ Openness

Being more open is often just a case of switching off autopilot and engaging fully with what's going on around you. For some people, autopilot includes an automatically negative and suspicious response to any new idea, person or situation, which can be very difficult to throw off. Take it slowly and you'll gradually get used to being more open.

▶ Vulnerability

Like openness, the willingness to be vulnerable can be difficult to retain in a pressured, busy lifestyle. Examine the boundaries that you set regarding your physical and emotional safety, and decide where you can allow yourself to be more vulnerable.

▶ Curiosity

There is nothing curious about autopilot mode, since on autopilot we notice very little and, as a result, miss very much. A mindful attitude brings curiosity to everything.

▶ Concentration

In everyday activities, this is a question of focus. Multitasking can seem like a great gift in a busy life but more often than not it means that many things are half done and nothing is properly done. Mindfulness asks you to focus on the task in hand and concentrate fully.

Preparing to be mindful

Sometimes you will be practising mindfulness while continuing with the task in hand. The whole point of this is to engage mindfully with the activity. At other times you'll choose to stop what you're doing in order to take a few minutes to get into Being mode. Be sure to make a firm decision one way or the other.

MINDFUL BREATHING

Whether you're undertaking a planned mindful activity or dealing with an unexpected need to be mindful, you should always start with a moment of mindful breathing. Think of this as grounding and centring both your mind and your body. It can also be very calming, although mindful breathing doesn't aim to calm you.

You can also practise mindful breathing throughout the day as a way of bringing yourself back to the present moment.

Try it now: Notice your breathing

Decide on a day for doing this exercise. Decide that at intervals throughout the day you will pause for a moment and bring your awareness to your breathing. Simply observe your breathing, which will vary according to what you're doing (slow if you're sitting at a desk, faster and deeper if you've just run upstairs) and how you're feeling (slow if you're calm, faster and shallower if you're tense). If you find it hard to remember to do this, you can use a timer or a random trigger. For example, you could aim to notice your breathing every time your phone rings, for two rings, and then answer it on the third ring.

EYES OPEN OR CLOSED?

However you have chosen to meditate for your long, private sessions, you need to consider what you do when carrying out mindfulness exercises in your everyday life. For instance, if you decide to take advantage of a red traffic light for a moment of mindful breathing, then you will need to keep your eyes open to monitor the lights. You also need to consider your own safety and that of others. On the whole, it's best to keep your eyes open.

Mindful activities

You can bring mindfulness to virtually any activity, from cleaning your teeth to servicing the car. The same principles apply whatever the activity is. Allow yourself to be fully engaged with the activity in the present moment, instead of doing it on autopilot while your mind is busy with other things. Be aware of distractions within the activity, though. For instance, if you're frying eggs and become mindfully engaged with the beauty of the yellow yolks, it's not very helpful if the eggs are burnt while you're engaged in that way.

Remember this

Mindful engagement on the wrong thing may be dangerous, for example if you're driving or using machinery. To do these activities mindfully, you need to be focused, not distracted.

DRIVING

Driving provides an interesting example of the power of mindfulness. A competent driver will be able to manage the mechanics of driving – steering, gear changing, etc. – on autopilot and this is appropriate, since it leaves your full attention available for driving safely. However, there are several aspects of driving where a mindful approach can make a driver both safer and less stressed:

▶ Take a moment before starting the engine to settle yourself into a mindful attitude.

▶ Open your awareness to include the traffic around you, as well as pedestrians and the road conditions.

▶ Maintain an awareness of your body, releasing any tensions that build up during traffic jams and other difficulties.

▶ Extend your awareness to other drivers, letting go of any competitiveness and taking a kindly attitude.

If everyone drove like this, how different our roads would be!

Self-assessment

Are there any activities in your life that would benefit from a mindful attitude towards them? Think of the things you enjoy doing as well as chores, and also include any regular task that you find particularly irksome. In your journal, make a list of activities to which you could bring a mindful approach.

Try it now: Do an activity mindfully

Take one activity from the list you made of your regular activities and try doing it mindfully. Work your way through the list.

Self-assessment

In your journal, keep notes of your responses to doing the various activities mindfully.

As well as targeting specific activities, you can bring mindfulness into play at any point during the day. Let's go back to that supermarket queue. You've rushed in there at a time when it's normally quiet, expecting to be in and out in a few moments. But something has gone wrong and there aren't enough tills open, so the queues are building up. Your stress levels start to rise, and yet there's nothing you can do – you need the items that are in your trolley.

Do you start to fume about the incompetence of the shop manager, or your own bad decision to leave the shopping till the last minute? Or do you stop and bring mindfulness into play? You would probably say that you were, indeed, living fully in the moment – too much so, since the moment was an annoying one. However, mindfulness also asks you to acknowledge and accept. As soon as you do so, your stress levels will start to fall. They'll fall even further if you also remember to be kind to yourself. The queue is long, you need the items, and there is nothing you can do. You had no way of knowing that this would happen, but it has and it's not your fault.

If you extend that kindness to other people, you'll find yourself thinking that the management probably do their best, the other people in the queue are just as fed up as you are (or at least as you were, until you remembered to be mindful) and the person on the checkout is having to work flat out to get through the queue quickly.

Try it now: Practise managing unexpected stress

If you practise mindfulness, you will be able to deal with unexpected stress mindfully. The next time you have an unexpectedly stressful situation, stop for a moment, bring your awareness to what's happening, acknowledge and accept what's happening and then allow a feeling of kindness to yourself and any other people involved.

Focus points

1 Regular meditation is the basis of mindfulness.
2 Everyday mindfulness doesn't require formal practice.
3 You can practise mindfulness anywhere, in any posture.
4 Be in the moment, accepting and kindly.
5 Have patience, openness and vulnerability.
6 Bring curiosity and concentration to everyday mindfulness.
7 Start with mindful breathing.
8 You can choose specific activities to carry out mindfully.
9 Some activities include an element of autopilot for safety.
10 You can be mindful at times of unexpected stress.

Next step

The next chapter explains some techniques for incorporating mindfulness into your everyday life.

11

Mindfulness in everyday life – techniques

In this chapter you will learn:

▶ *the various ways to start each day mindfully*
▶ *how to do a three-minute breathing space*
▶ *how to do mini meditations and body scans*
▶ *formal and informal ways of moving mindfully*
▶ *about the benefits of everyday mindfulness.*

Starting the day

It's a good idea to start each day mindfully. There are various ways to do this, so choose the ones that fit best with your routine. You can:

▶ wake up early and do a full meditation

▶ wake up early and do mindful stretching or yoga

▶ wake up at your usual time but allow yourself to come to gradually, noticing the small sounds, sights and smells of the new day

▶ be mindful for three breaths when you first wake up

▶ be mindful during your bath or shower.

▶ be mindful while you eat your breakfast.

Three-minute breathing space

The three-minute breathing space was devised as part of using mindfulness in therapy, but it's a useful tool for anyone who wants to be more mindful in everyday life. We all tend to take breathing spaces throughout the day without necessarily realizing it, but this is a more formal way of structuring a tiny break that will send you back to your tasks with renewed energy.

If you observe other people, you'll soon notice their breathing spaces – a coffee, a toilet break, even a cigarette. In fact, anyone trying to give up smoking is well advised to find alternative ways of creating breathing spaces rather than trying to do without them at all.

The three-minute breathing space has three components, and as long as you include all three you can actually make it shorter than three minutes. Even three breaths will give you a breathing space, if you use one breath for each component.

Before you start a three-minute breathing space, stop what you're doing. This is obviously necessary for some activities where safety is concerned (driving, operating machinery), but even if you're just at your desk, you do need to stop for the duration of the breathing space and give it your full attention.

The three stages follow a pattern:

▶ **Stage one** creates an awareness of your whole being as it is at that moment.

▶ **Stage two** brings your awareness in to the small area of your abdomen where your breathing is centred.

▶ **Stage three** opens your awareness back out into your whole body, creating calmness and energy.

STAGE 1: AWARENESS

The first step is to take your awareness into your particular present moment. This means switching off your autopilot and checking in with yourself. Briefly take your awareness to your breathing. Check your body, and accept any sensations, whether pleasant or uncomfortable. Also check any part of your body that you know, from your practice of the body scan, is likely to be carrying your emotions physically. Become aware of your thoughts and try to disengage from them. Finally, take your awareness to your emotions and accept them, whether good or bad.

This sounds like a lot to cover in one minute, or one breath, but your regular practice will make these checks so familiar that you'll be able to run through them quickly.

STAGE 2: BREATHING

Take your full attention to your breathing, and observe it without trying to change it. (If you feel it changing as a natural consequence of stopping what you were doing, that's fine. Observe that too.) Pay particular attention to your stomach and feel your breath moving in and out of your body.

STAGE 3: EXPANDING AWARENESS

The third step is to let your awareness expand out from your stomach, using your breathing as your guide. Let yourself breathe into the rest of your body and feel the peaceful energy that breath delivers.

Mini meditations

The three-minute breathing space is a kind of mini meditation. You can also do less structured mini meditations throughout the day. Again, it is the regular, longer sessions that will give you the ability to do these: to switch off autopilot, let go of Doing and drop quickly into Being mode by taking your awareness to your breathing. If you have a fairly structured day, you can programme in times for these mini sessions. It's particularly useful when you're switching activities, for instance at the beginning and end of your work lunch-break, or when you go from work to family life. You can also use mini meditations at any time.

Mini body scan

You've already seen how you bring your awareness to your body during the three-minute breathing space, and you can also use short body-scan sessions throughout the day. It's another way of providing a breathing space, or creating a bridge between various activities. Your experience of doing longer, full body scans will have taught you where in your body you carry your daily tensions, and for a short body scan you should concentrate on those areas.

Try it now: Do a mini body scan

From your longer body-scan practice, decide where in your body you carry your tension. The most common areas are shoulders, neck, chest and stomach. You don't need a special posture, but you do need to stop what you're doing for a moment and take your awareness to your breathing. Then, as you breathe in, feel the breath travelling to the part, or parts, of your body. As you breathe out, allow the tension to leave with the breath.

Everyday mindful movement

Most of the things we do require movement, and much of the time we are on autopilot. With everyday mindful movement, you'll be combining an awareness of movement with an awareness of the task itself.

There are two kinds of everyday mindful movement, formal and informal:

▶ **Formal everyday mindful movement**

This is where you carry out tasks slowly, thoughtfully and with total focus, just as you did with formal mindful walking (see Chapter 8). Be aware of your body, the movements it needs to make, and the task itself – for instance, the shape and colour of an onion, the smell released as you cut into it, and so on.

Try it now: Formal mindful movement

Use the list you created in Chapter 10 and choose simple tasks from it, as these are the ones you're most likely to do on autopilot. Choose a specific task to do in a formal, mindful way. As you'll probably feel self-conscious, choose something you can do in private. Start with a task that you find enjoyable, such as cooking, and later move on to something that is purely a chore, such as, in my case, dusting.

▶ **Informal everyday mindful movement**

This involves choosing specific tasks to carry out with your full attention and engagement, but without the super-slowness of formal mindful movement. If you proceed mindfully you are likely to find, though, that you are a little slower and more thorough than you would otherwise be. Your focus will be on your body and the movements it needs to make in order to complete the task.

If you do a task that you find particularly challenging or tedious, you may well find that doing it mindfully helps the time to pass more easily. Dusting mindfully is a challenge for me, but strangely I do find that the time passes more easily and also that I'm reminded of the beauty of the wooden furniture that I'm lucky enough to own.

Try it now: Informal mindful movement

Repeat your tasks (or choose different ones) but allow yourself to move at a more normal speed. Remember to be fully engaged with the physical aspects of the task, giving them your full attention.

Self-assessment

How did it feel to do the exercises? Make notes on what you discovered. You will find your own benefits in mindful movement, and you might be surprised to find emotional release, or emotional responses to the tasks, occurring. Our tendency to rush busily from one task to the next will often throw a blanket over our emotions, which emerge only when we slow down and work mindfully. Allow this to happen, observe the emotions with detachment, and let them be as they need to be.

Benefits of everyday mindfulness

Bringing mindfulness into your everyday life will create practical and obvious benefits, as opposed to the more subtle benefits of regular meditation. You'll learn what works for you, and you'll learn that bringing your attention into the present moment through the various activities gives you a range of mindful choices, each one helpful in a different way. By constantly checking in with your body you'll learn more about how your mind and body interact, and you'll strengthen that relationship.

Gradually, you'll find that even the most routine activities become more satisfying if performed mindfully, and pleasurable activities become even more pleasurable. You may find that you have more energy, because Being mode allows you to recharge your batteries.

You'll also find yourself dealing with difficulties in a more mindful way. If you're able to take a step back and detach yourself from experiences, observing them rather than engaging with them, you'll achieve a new perspective. Instead of reacting in a knee-jerk way, you'll find time to reflect (even a few moments can be enough if they are mindful moments) and produce a considered response.

Remember that example of someone being rude to you on the phone? We looked at reactions such as being rude right back or bursting into tears. A mindful approach would be quite different. You would be aware of their rudeness and also of your own emotional response, but you wouldn't necessarily act on it. Instead, you could stay focused on the reason for the phone call. Anyone who has studied assertiveness already knows how to do this. Mindfulness gives you the same skills, and also allows you to detach from your own emotions.

Overcoming challenges

You may find that you feel incorporating mindfulness into your everyday life is just a step too far, for several reasons.

LACK OF TIME

It's one thing to set aside a specific time each day for mindful meditation – rather like starting an evening class or a new hobby, your initial enthusiasm carries you forward, and the designated times become part of your routine – but the rest of the time you feel that you are too busy and mindfulness makes you too slow. In fact, you may feel that you have to rush even more in order to make the time for your daily meditation sessions. If this is the case for you, take it gradually and ease yourself slowly into everyday mindfulness.

Key idea

Give priority to your formal meditation at first, and gradually work your way through the exercises in this chapter. There's no hurry.

FEAR OF CHANGE

Have you accepted the idea of learning to meditate, but still see it as something separate from your main or real life? Perhaps everyday mindfulness seems a little threatening, as if it were going to take over everything. Again, take your time, and allow yourself to gradually get used to this new way of doing things.

LACK OF ENERGY

Many of us rush through each day in a whirlwind of energy, sustained by caffeine and sugar, only to collapse in a heap at the end of the day, sleep for a few hours and then start the whole thing all over again the next day. The idea of stopping for any sort of break in the middle of the day can be scary, because you may well feel that once you stop you'll never have the energy to get started again. If you have this fear, then ease yourself in gradually. Do your first few exercises at times when it wouldn't be too catastrophic if you fell asleep or found that you couldn't get started again. As you gain confidence in the energizing power of mindfulness, you can gradually extend it into your busiest times.

DIFFICULT EMOTIONS

You may be concerned that if a difficult emotion surfaces during a mini meditation you won't be able to cope with it, and that it could interfere with your day. This is another reason why you start by establishing a habit of daily meditation. During these sessions you'll discover both whether your emotions do surface during meditation and also how to stay detached from them, observing but not engaging. If you find that you have many emotional issues to work through during your formal meditation sessions, then take your time over incorporating mini meditations into your everyday life.

Focus points

1 Start the day mindfully.
2 Practise the three-minute breathing space.
3 Remember: Awareness, Breathing and Calmness.
4 Use mini meditations throughout the day.
5 Use mini body scans at times of stress.
6 Practise everyday tasks with mindful movement.
7 Mindfulness increases the chance of flow in everyday activities.
8 Everyday mindfulness helps you deal with difficulties.
9 Accept that you may resist being mindful in daily life.
10 Don't use mini meditations if you find that difficult emotions tend to surface.

Next step

The next chapter describes various mindfulness tools you can use and tells you how to implement the eight-week course model for establishing a regular routine that works for you.

12

Your mindfulness programme

In this chapter you will learn:

▶ *how to bring the various mindfulness tools into your life*

▶ *how to implement an eight-week model for your mindfulness practice*

▶ *how to practise mindful detachment.*

I was always puzzled that every day my high-flying, go-getting neighbour went straight out to his fishpond as soon as he got home from work, in all weathers. I asked what it was that he had to do for the fish each day, and he said, 'Nothing. I just look at them.' It was his way of being mindful for a few moments.

Key idea

Even a few short moments of peace and quietness every day will improve your quality of life.

Mindfulness in essence is very simple. It's a question of being fully present in the moment, accepting whatever the moment brings, and having a non-judgemental attitude of kindliness. It turns out, though, that simple doesn't always mean easy, and the exercises in the previous chapters will have shown you this. You've begun to learn about yourself through doing the exercises; you know what is easy for you and what you find difficult, what is pleasurable and what throws up challenges.

You may also be feeling that there are too many choices, too many different ways to practise mindfulness and to incorporate it into your life. Any new activity can seem overwhelming at first, but continued practice brings familiarity and you start to feel more comfortable with it.

The core of mindfulness is a meditation session once or twice daily, and this is where you should start. You can bring other practices into your life one at a time, allowing the appropriate moment to make itself felt.

When you create a mindful way of life for yourself, it's important to make it realistic and to keep to it, rather than set overly high expectations and fail to keep them. If you can find only a few minutes a day, then start with that and discover the benefits of keeping to your intention.

Remember this

Whatever you do, try to create a routine so that it becomes automatic to meet your commitment.

An eight-week course in mindfulness

When mindfulness is used in a clinical setting, the courses usually run for eight weeks, so if you prefer a more structured approach you can follow this eight-week model. Each week you try a different aspect of mindfulness practice, and at the end of the time you will have a feel for what works for you, so that you can establish a regular routine. There are various ways of structuring the eight weeks. You could, for instance, take Chapters 2, 3, 4, 5, 6, 7, 8 and 10 of this book and work through one chapter each week. Alternatively, here is a structure that is rather closer to the way mindfulness is used in therapy:

▶ **Week 1** – Read about automatic pilot. Try eating a raisin mindfully. Read about body scan.

▶ **Week 2** – Try a body scan. Read about mindful breathing. Try being mindful during one routine activity each day.

▶ **Week 3** – Learn about mindful movement. Try mindful stretching. Read about the three-minute breathing space.

▶ **Week 4** – Try other types of mindful movement. Read more about mindful attention. Try a short sitting meditation. Practise a three-minute breathing space three times a day, and also when coping with difficult times.

▶ **Week 5** – Read about acceptance and detachment. Try a longer sitting meditation. Continue with the three-minute breathing space.

▶ **Week 6** – Read about accepting that thoughts are not facts. Sitting meditation extended to at least 30 minutes. Three-minute breathing space continued.

▶ **Week 7** – Read about nurturing yourself. Sitting meditation every day. Three-minute breathing space continued.

▶ **Week 8** – Revisit the body scan. Sitting meditation every day. Three-minute breathing space continued.

However you choose to do it, it's crucially important to set your intention and stick with it for all the formal practices. It's far less effective if you suddenly decide you've got five minutes so you might as well do a quick meditation – this is OK for a mini meditation or a three-minute breathing space, but not for your main daily session or sessions.

Remember this

Your central commitment is to daily meditation, with other practices to be added gradually.

If there is something that you don't want to do right now, then make a decision to return to it later. This is better than making a half-hearted commitment to something that you probably won't get round to. Here is a list to help you make sure you've considered everything:

1 Sitting meditation – breathing

2 Sitting meditation – loving-kindness

3 Body scan

4 Mindful movement – formal and informal

5 Mindful stretching

6 Mindful walking – formal and informal

7 Mindfulness in everyday activities

8 Three-minute breathing space

9 Mini meditations

10 Mini body scan

Self-assessment

Decide how you want to structure your mindfulness practice and write it down in your journal. Make a contract with yourself to meet this commitment.

Mindful detachment

You've probably heard the expression 'wake up and smell the roses' (or, sometimes, 'wake up and smell the coffee'). It's another way of reminding you to switch off the autopilot and engage with the moment, which often has intense pleasures to offer you if only you would notice them. Mindfulness itself is not goal-driven or pleasure-oriented, but it's important to experience the actual journey of mindfulness without worrying too much about the destination – just smell the roses by the wayside. Not every meditation will feel good, and not every exercise will have a positive result, but if you remember to stay detached and observant of all your responses then you'll find that you can engage with the journey, and you can let go of worrying about goals and success or failure.

Self-assessment

What were your goals when you started reading this book? Did you have expectations of mindfulness? Did you want to achieve certain things? Write them down in your journal.

Try it now: Practise detachment

Sit comfortably and breathe mindfully for a few moments. When your mind and body have settled, bring your attention to the goals you noted in your journal. Accept whatever expectations you had for mindfulness, and detach from them.

DETACHMENT FROM THOUGHTS

This ability to observe and detach will also help you reach an understanding about your thoughts. We seem to be able to fully understand that some thoughts are fleeting and have no basis in fact. For instance, minor irritations about a person, or a job, that you love are recognized as temporary, even as they're happening. You still love the person or job and you know the irritation will pass.

We also know that a thought can seem to be true and yet can be quickly disproven. For instance, most of us have had the experience of struggling to master something, and having the despondent thought 'I'll never get the hang of this' and yet after a few repetitions it miraculously becomes easy.

Despite all this evidence, almost everyone has some thoughts that seem to them to be absolute truth. Often these are self-critical thoughts, such as 'I'm useless' or 'I always make a fool of myself' or 'I never have any luck'. It seems likely that this type of thought is created very early in childhood (therapists call them 'core beliefs') so that they seem more like universal truths than just thoughts. If your core beliefs are deeply negative, as in the examples, then you're likely to find life difficult. Mindful detachment, acceptance and kindness to yourself can all help you let go of negative core beliefs.

Negative thoughts of all types can be part of what Buddhists call the 'second arrow of suffering'. The idea behind this is that if you are struck by an arrow it hurts, but if you then allow yourself to become distressed and despondent about the pain then you are doubling your suffering. The same is true of mental suffering. If something distressing happens, it hurts emotionally, but if you add a whole layer of negative thoughts to your sadness you've doubled your emotional pain. No one can avoid the first arrow; every life has bad things in it, but mindful detachment will help you avoid the second arrow of unnecessary suffering.

There is more about this in Part two. For now, concentrate on establishing your regular mindful meditation practice and on familiarizing yourself with the other mindfulness techniques.

Focus points

1 Mindfulness is simple but not always easy.
2 Trying mindfulness for eight weeks gives you time to decide which approaches best suit you.
3 Be realistic.
4 Meditation isn't always pleasurable.
5 Create an intention and stick to it.
6 Meditate every day.
7 Mindfulness is not about pleasure or achieving goals.
8 Let go of your expectations.
9 Detach from your thoughts.
10 Detach from your emotions.

Next step

Taking time to nurture yourself is essential for well-being, and the next chapter suggests how you can do this by taking just one day to practise mindfulness.

13

Taking time for yourself

In this chapter you will learn:

▶ *why it is important to nurture yourself*
▶ *about the idea of taking a mindfulness retreat*
▶ *how to approach a day of mindfulness.*

Imagine someone walking by a fast-flowing river. Suddenly, they slip on the mud and fall in. Two people rush to help. The first one leaps in and grabs the person who fell in, but they can't swim strongly enough to make it back to the bank. So now two people are in trouble in the water. Luckily, the second rescuer has taken the extra time to find the safety equipment that's on the riverbank. They tie one end of the rope to a tree, checking it for firmness, and then throw the life ring out to the two people in the water. They grab hold of it. The rescuer finds a place on the bank that isn't muddy, gets a firm footing and hauls on the rope, slowly but steadily bringing the people back to the bank.

It's obvious that the second rescuer was the most effective – they were able to help while still staying safe on the bank.

Very few of us will ever have to make a decision about the best way to help someone who has fallen in a river, but we may well end up trying to help people who are struggling in their lives. If you were going through a hard time, who would you rather turn to, someone who was grounded and sorted, or someone who was trying to cope with the burden of their own issues?

The point is that taking time for yourself isn't selfish; it's essential if you are going to function well in your relationships. Whether you're a parent or a boss (or both), you will be more able to care for others if you start by caring for yourself.

Taking just one day

With this in mind, consider the option of taking one whole day to practise mindfulness. It's best to do this a few weeks or even months into your regular meditation practice, so that some of the newness and strangeness has worn off, and you're at least beginning to feel a sense of familiarity with it. You'll also have experienced any difficulties that meditation might throw up for you, and begun to find ways to overcome them. If meditation has already released some difficult emotions, you'll have had a chance to experience that and cope with it.

Some mindfulness teachers recommend taking a day every single week for mindfulness, and while that would be wonderful, for most of us it simply isn't practical. So aim for one day, just one day, to find out how it feels.

Don't rush into setting this up: take your time and make sure you've covered all the aspects of your life, from childcare to shopping. You may have to make arrangements with other people, and the day may have to be one that harmonizes with their schedule.

Remember this

Even if you think your life is too full of responsibilities to be able take time away from them, it is often possible to ask a close friend or partner to take over for just one day. There was a period in my life when I felt I couldn't take a day for myself, as I was responsible for my elderly father who often phoned needing something from me. It was a breakthrough moment when I realized that I could ask a trusted friend to deal with the calls for just one day.

Mindfulness retreats

Mindfulness retreats offer us an opportunity to nurture ourselves in a supportive environment. Often led by Buddhist monks, such retreats allow you to take time out from your life and develop calmness and clarity. There is a cost involved, and while some are for longer than a day, a day retreat is a good place to start.

You should expect that, although there will be other people present, you will spend the day in silence, and much of your time alone. Retreats do not require any previous experience of mindfulness, but they will deepen and extend whatever you have already learned.

Do check out the organization before you sign up for a retreat, and make sure the teacher is experienced. Look at the programme and see whether it looks right for you – some retreats are more rigorous than others. A silent retreat could be difficult for people in emotional distress, and it could be easier to develop mindfulness in a setting where there are more possibilities for active engagement. The least challenging retreats combine a schedule of meditation with time for a holiday, although these are usually for longer than one day.

Key idea

There is a variety of mindfulness retreats to choose from: some are Buddhist-based and others are completely secular; some are based in the countryside and on farms, while others are in urban areas. See Taking it further and use the Internet to find out whether there's a centre near you.

Creating your own retreat

It can be very beneficial to create a day of mindfulness in your own home. You'll feel safe in familiar surroundings and, although at first you may feel that your everyday life is pressing in on you, you'll actually learn ways of detaching yourself from it, which will be helpful to your long-term mindfulness practice.

The key practical requirements for a day of mindfulness are as follows:

▶ This is a day entirely for you, spent largely in silence.

▶ As far as possible you will be alone, and people around you need to understand that you won't be meeting any of their demands.

▶ You will keep all phones, computers and electronic gadgets switched off. In case you were wondering, this does include television and radio.

▶ There should be no novels, factual books, newspapers or magazines.

▶ You will arrange food and other necessities beforehand.

▶ You won't need your journal for this exercise.

A day of mindfulness

Here is a suggestion for the shape of a mindful day, but you can choose to organize your day differently.

1 The day actually starts at bedtime the night before. You can fall asleep with mindful breathing, secure in the knowledge that you have an entire day of Being ahead of you. Don't set an alarm; you don't need one, and you can sleep as much or as little as your body demands.

2 When you wake up, take a few moments to connect with yourself. There's no need to leap out of bed and hit the ground running, so focus on your breathing and gradually re-enter the world.

3 When you decide to get out of bed, stand up slowly, staying in contact with your breathing. Spend a few moments looking at something pleasurable – a picture, or the view from your window, especially if you can see sky and natural objects. Have a drink and perhaps a piece of fruit – nothing heavy just yet. Take your time over preparing and eating these, then decide either to meditate with a breathing meditation or do a body scan.

4 Have a bath or shower, and get dressed, slowly and mindfully. You have a whole day, remember. Follow this with breakfast, prepared and eaten mindfully. You can spend the morning on small household tasks, such as clearing away the breakfast things and making the bed, or gardening. Don't launch yourself into a spring clean or a major clearout. Do each thing mindfully, fully present and engaged with the task, not rushing to get it over with. If you prefer, you can do some walking meditation. By all means stop for a tea break, and linger over your drink so that you really taste it. Use the three-minute breathing space from time to time, perhaps when you've finished one activity and before you start another.

5 Take your time preparing your lunch, mindfully. This will be your main meal of the day, so allow yourself to take it slowly, eating every mouthful mindfully. Afterwards, you

might like to rest a little, while you digest the meal, and then choose an activity. This can be something you enjoy, such as a hobby, or some mindful stretching if you prefer. Yoga or t'ai chi are good if you enjoy either of these.

6 In the early evening do another formal meditation before you eat something light. Good evening activities are writing, or reading poetry, religious texts or anything you find inspirational. You can meditate before bedtime, but if you find meditation too energizing then do it earlier in the evening. This can be a good time to meditate on the topic of gratitude. Let your mind focus on all the good things in your life (enough to eat, a place to live, family, friends, good health – create your own list) and be grateful for them. Don't dwell on anything that isn't quite right in your life – there is plenty of time for that on other days. Depending on where you are, a quiet evening stroll can be a good preparation for bed.

7 Finally, fall asleep with mindful focus on your breathing.

Potential challenges

The first exercise in this book asked you to do nothing for two minutes, and it's a long journey from that to a whole day of mindfulness. For that reason, a day of mindfulness probably won't all be plain sailing, and it will help to look at the potential difficulties and challenges.

THOUGHTS
Once you're fully awake, your normal habit of always having to think about the next thing, along with many other thoughts hovering in the background, may well try to assert itself. Don't beat yourself up about having thoughts: gently bring your mind back to the present moment.

You may also find that, as the day progresses and you start to feel your mind as a wide open space, it feels quite natural to start thinking about all the things that you don't normally have time for. These are often quite big topics – planning the trip of a lifetime, wondering whether you're in the right job or the right relationship and so on. A day of mindfulness can seem like the ideal opportunity to tackle these big questions, but your challenge is to treat these thoughts like any others, and gently bring your mind back to the present moment. Remind yourself that it's a day of rest from thinking.

BOREDOM

It's probably a long time since you had a whole day of just Being – perhaps not since you were a tiny baby – and at some point your mind might start to complain of boredom. As far as possible, treat these thoughts like any others, and gently guide your mind back to the present moment. It might help to think of your mind as being like a toddler, easily distracted, and in need of an adult to quietly take it away from the distraction.

RESTLESSNESS

At some point during the day, you may well start to feel that you've recharged your batteries quite enough and are ready to get busy again. This is another trick of your mind, which is trying to get back to Doing mode. Remind yourself that you decided to make it a whole day of mindfulness, and that sticking to your intention is an important mindfulness skill.

EMOTIONS

As the day progresses and your mind opens and clears, you may find various emotions coming to the fore. These are not likely to be new emotions, but rather emotions that have been crowded out by all the clamour and busyness of daily life. Remember to observe them calmly, with detachment, so that they don't overwhelm you. Most emotions are short-lived, like a wave that washes over you and is gone. However important such emotions may seem, you don't have to engage with them during your day of mindfulness, and you'll be more able to deal with any issues that are driving them after your day of mindfulness.

Try it now: Spend a mindful day

Spend a mindful day, either following the suggested programme described above or adapting it as you wish to suit you.

Focus points

1 You need to look after yourself before you can look after others.
2 A whole day of mindfulness is your gift to yourself.
3 Wait until at least a few weeks into your practice before you spend a mindful day.
4 Consider going on an organized retreat.
5 Consider creating your own retreat.
6 Arrange to be alone for the day.
7 Arrange food and anything else you need beforehand.
8 Explain what you are undertaking to other people beforehand.
9 Turn off the phone, television, computer and so on.
10 Don't read any novels, magazines, newspapers or factual books.

Next step

In the next section of the book we'll look at how mindfulness can help you achieve a more balanced relationship with yourself and how it can be applied to specific aspects of life.

Part two

Applying mindfulness skills

14

Mindfulness: a way of life

In this chapter you will learn:

▶ *why people choose to live mindfully*
▶ *more about the 'second arrow of suffering'*
▶ *about the concept of the self.*

In its pure Buddhist form, mindfulness has no aims, goals or practical applications. It is just a way of living your life. Of course, there are reasons for choosing to live mindfully. Buddhists believe, among other things, that we are all suffering, and that mindfulness offers us a way to let go of suffering (which includes physical pain as well as mental suffering such as unhappiness and self-destructive behaviour). They believe that we all yearn to escape from suffering and that mindful meditation and living mindfully will help us do this and move us towards happiness.

The 'second arrow of suffering'

As the concept of mindfulness has moved into Western culture, it has inevitably been changed and influenced by that culture, but the idea that mindful living can help us eliminate or minimize our suffering has remained. You already know a little about the valuable Buddhist concept known as the 'second arrow of suffering', which is a way of describing the suffering we create in our own minds.

Let's look at the example of the rudeness on the phone scenario. The first arrow is the incident of someone being rude to you. It hurts, no doubt about it. But the second arrow is the pain you feel if you react with anger or defensiveness, and the pain that continues afterwards when you beat yourself up for either losing your temper or not standing up for yourself. It is mindfulness that can really help you learn to let go of this second arrow. You can't stop someone from being rude to you, just as you can't stop most of the bad things that happen in life, but you can do something about your reactions to them. The mindful idea is that, by detaching yourself from your thoughts and emotions, by accepting that both are fleeting and changeable, you can release yourself from their power to make you unhappy.

Key idea

While we can't stop bad things from happening in life, we can control how we react to them. By practising detachment, we can let go of our negative thoughts and emotions.

This can seem like a very difficult concept to many of us in the Western world. We value our emotions and our engagement with them, and we tend to assume that 'I am my thoughts'. Ironically, both of these concepts are comparatively recent developments in our culture – before the Romantic movement of the late eighteenth century it would probably have been much easier for Westerners to understand mindfulness. Romanticism emphasized the importance of the individual as opposed to the group, and the importance of each individual's unique inner life, and here we are 250 years later still living with the consequences of that emphasis.

Like any great cultural movement, Romanticism brought with it both advantages and disadvantages. One potential disadvantage is that it's possible to become over-focused on oneself. I used to spend a lot of time worrying about the future, in both big and small ways. It wasn't until I began to understand mindfulness that I also began to understand my grandfather's favourite saying: 'Don't cross your bridges till you come to them.'

It's easy to recognize the person who is self-obsessed and relates everything back to their own needs, but it's also true that people who constantly insist, 'Never mind me, I'm not important,' are also making the self too important – just in a different way.

Psychoanalysis, therapies and counselling are all part of our general post-Romantic fascination with the self, and there's no doubt that they've been very helpful to very many people. Over the last two decades, mindfulness has become part of this toolbox, since it offers ways of taking a step back and freeing ourselves from self-obsession.

The concept of the self

If you've ever been around a newborn baby, you know that they have no sense of self and no concept that they are a separate entity. It comes as a horrible revelation to them when they are a few months old and they suddenly realize that their mother, or main carer, is able to go away and leave them. We call this 'separation anxiety' and it is a stage that all children pass through, until they gradually learn that they can manage life on their own.

As part of this process, children go through a stage of being intensely self-centred before reaching the more balanced position of adulthood. However, once we're launched on adult life, usually in virtually permanent Doing mode, we rarely stop to think that we may not have reached the end of the journey.

Mindfulness offers a way of continuing to develop your relationship with yourself (and remember that this relationship needs to be well grounded before you can have good relationships with other people). Meditation can seem intensely introspective to an outside observer, but in fact mindful meditation is a process of learning to let go of your self, and opening yourself up to connections with other people. The loving-kindness meditation is a particularly important part of the process. Ultimately, you'll regain the newborn baby's sense that each of us is a part of everything in the universe.

This brings with it a wonderful sense of liberation, like a weight being lifted, and actually makes it easier for you to be comfortable in your own skin.

Remember this

When we become mindful, we let go of our self-obsession and become more connected to other people and more aware of our place in the universe.

Focus points

1 Mindfulness is a way of living.
2 Buddhists believe that we are all suffering but yearn for happiness.
3 We create the 'second arrow of suffering' in our own minds.
4 You are not your emotions.
5 You are not your thoughts.
6 Babies don't have a sense of a separate identity.
7 Adults can lose their sense of connectedness with everything.
8 Meditation takes you into yourself but also back out into the universe.
9 Regaining the sense of connectedness is very liberating.
10 Mindfulness helps you re-establish connectedness.

Next step

You will learn more in the next chapter about using mindfulness in everyday life: for energy, for listening, for managing a stressful situation or a crisis, and for improving the quality of your sleep.

15

Mindfulness in daily life

In this chapter you will learn:

▶ *how to meditate for energy*
▶ *how to listen mindfully*
▶ *about using mindfulness for crisis management*
▶ *how to improve your sleep pattern.*

You've already seen in Part one how you can start to use mindfulness in your everyday life, but you can also bring it to bear on specific everyday difficulties, the kind of things we all have to face from time to time.

Meditation for energy

One of the bonuses of meditation for most people is an increase in available energy. Sometimes this effect is felt immediately after meditating; for others it's an effect of the whole mindfulness programme. You will find that you use your energy more efficiently. Maintaining physical tension absorbs energy to no purpose, and a regular body scan will help you release any tension you carry, freeing up that energy.

Mindful awareness of your body will also teach you how your energy levels change, and you may begin to see connections – for example, missing breakfast may lead you to have low energy levels later in the morning. You'll become more in touch with the natural ebb and flow of your energy.

Self-assessment

Keep a record in your journal of your energy levels for a few days to help see the bigger picture.

Mindfulness isn't a shortcut – you'll still need to look after yourself energy-wise, by:

▶ eating regularly

▶ avoiding sugar

▶ exercising regularly

▶ drinking enough water

▶ managing your stress.

Carrying out a three-minute breathing space can give you a quick energy boost, or you can do the following longer meditation specifically aimed at raising your energy levels.

Try it now: Meditate for energy

You don't need a special posture for this, but do make sure you are comfortable. Stop whatever you're doing so that you can give the meditation your full attention.

Pay mindful attention to your breathing for a few breaths. When you feel your mind starting to settle, take your focus to your diaphragm and feel how it powers your breathing. Imagine that, as you breathe in, you take in useful energy and, as you breathe out, you let go of negative thoughts and toxins. Do this for several breaths.

Now move on to feeling the energy move through your body. Each time you breathe in, imagine that the energy makes you glow, a little more each time, spreading out from your middle, until the gentle glow of energy has suffused your entire body. Spend a little time bathing in the glow of the energy, feeling how each in-breath creates more and more energy.

Gently bring your awareness back to your surroundings, allow yourself to reconnect with the world and carry on with your day, now with fully recharged batteries.

Mindful listening

One of the great casualties of Doing mode is often that we forget to listen. Every parent knows that small children will often choose the moment when you're late and trying to get out of the door to tell you something really important. It can be so hard to let go of your Doing-mode goal of getting there on time and switch to making time and space for the child to talk.

Adults, too, often have what counsellors call 'door-knob moments'. At the end of a session when, as they have their hand on the handle about to open the door and leave, they suddenly say something really important that's been on their mind for the whole hour. When I was the appointments clerk at a busy antenatal clinic, patients would often not mention a worry about their pregnancy until they were talking to me about their next appointment and about to leave. The medical staff would always keep a little time in hand to take those patients back into the clinic to discuss these worries.

Mindful listening is a great skill. It can improve relationships and make you more effective in the workplace. Its key requirements are:

▶ to be fully present in the conversation, letting go of any other thoughts

▶ to pay full attention to what the other person is saying

▶ not to think about what you're going to say next while they're speaking

▶ to let go of any negative feelings you may have about what they're saying

▶ to take your time when it's your turn to speak and consider what you're going to say.

You will find that mindful listening is a powerful tool in all situations where you need to connect with other people. If you have a tendency to judge people hastily, going by their appearance or their speech, then mindful listening will help you set that aside and connect with the real person behind the appearance.

Reacting and responding

A reaction happens automatically, without thought and quite quickly. A response is measured and considered. It may take fractionally longer to respond rather than react, but you will avoid the many pitfalls of the knee-jerk reaction. Anger, impatience, selfishness and greed are all likely to come to the fore if you react automatically.

Try it now: Recall your reaction to a past situation

Sit or lie quietly and take a few moments for mindful breathing. Spend some time recreating in your mind what happened the last time you reacted to a situation without thinking first. Try to really bring it to life by remembering the little details – what people were wearing, what time of day it was, what the weather was like and so on. Try to recreate the sensations you had at the time, and where in your body you felt them.

Self-assessment

How did that feel? Is it comfortable to recall yourself reacting like that? Can you honestly say that your reaction produced a good result? Almost always, the answer is no.

Try it now: Respond mindfully

Sit or lie quietly and take a few moments for mindful breathing. Recreate in your mind the scene you recalled in the previous exercise, again bringing it to life as much as you can. Now imagine yourself behaving mindfully, by staying in the moment but detached from your own knee-jerk reactions. What are the differences in your response?

Self-assessment

How did that feel? Of course, you will never know what might have happened if you had responded mindfully instead of reacting thoughtlessly, but ask yourself whether you'd feel more comfortable about your behaviour if you'd responded mindfully instead of reacting without thinking.

Crisis management

If you feel things starting to go wrong during the day, take a moment for a three-minute breathing space or a mini meditation. If you're in a public place, keep your eyes open, but allow yourself to take the time to mindfully re-centre yourself. Detaching from the panicky, anxious or angry feelings that come with an unexpected crisis can help you cope with it far better, so it's time well spent.

In a really stressful situation, such as a confrontation, you can still find a moment to bring yourself back to mindfulness. Let go of any need to react quickly and thoughtlessly and allow the space of one outward breath to calm yourself down – as you breathe out let go of any feelings of anger and defensiveness. Taking that mental step back may even be enough to defuse the situation. If you feel the need to say something during that moment, use a holding remark that will create space such as:

> 'Hang on a minute, let's just think about this.'

> 'Can you explain exactly what the problem is?'

For managing confrontation, we're often advised to use the acronym STOP, which is really mindfulness by another name:

▶ *S*ignal: your body sends you early-warning signals when things are going wrong, such as a tight throat or a rumbling stomach. Body scans will make you far more aware of your own personal signals. Once you're aware of them, it becomes easier to let go of them.

▶ *T*ake control: breathe mindfully for a few breaths.

▶ *O*pposite: as you feel your muscles go tense and your thoughts turn negative (from fear or aggression), take the opposite position, by deliberately relaxing and saying to yourself 'I am calm and in control.' This is mindful detachment from your negative reactions.

▶ *P*ractise: prepare yourself to practise these techniques when you know in advance that things might get difficult, for instance when you're returning something unsatisfactory to a shop or having to deal with a difficulty at work. Then, when an unexpected difficulty arises, you'll have the skills at your fingertips.

Remember this

Don't save mindfulness just for crises or confrontations – it needs to be a well-established part of your life before you'll be able to call on it at short notice.

Connecting with nature

Our increasingly urban existence takes us away from nature, and yet at the same time we recognize how badly we need that connection. Even a bunch of cut flowers or a pot plant on a desk can make us feel better about the day. In your mindfulness practice, connect with nature whenever you can, by:

▶ meditating out of doors whenever possible

▶ walking mindfully in a park, at the beach or in countryside

▶ being in your garden, if you have one, or a park or other open space, and being mindfully aware of the daily changes that the seasons bring

▶ bringing nature indoors with natural objects and plants

▶ remembering to look up at the sky and mindfully observe the changes in it.

Key idea

If at all possible, spend at least part of your work lunch-break in the open air. Even in an urban environment this will benefit you – be sure to look at the sky.

Sleeping well

It's important to get enough sleep, and to sleep well. Whatever problems you're experiencing will seem worse if you're tired, and your capacity to think clearly and make good decisions will be reduced. When you were trying out the exercises in Part one, did you find that the minute you stopped Doing you fell asleep? This is a sure sign that your current sleep regime isn't working as it should. You may be fully aware of this, or even suffering from insomnia, but equally you may feel that you sleep well without realizing that your mind is still busily racing.

Self-assessment

It can be helpful to keep a sleep diary for a week or two. It will show you what your pattern is and exactly how much sleep you're getting.

You may be surprised to find that you're getting more sleep than you thought – feeling tired and worrying about sleep can become a habit. It's also possible to sleep too much – for some people sleep becomes a retreat from life's problems, which is another form of avoidance.

AIDS TO SLEEP

There are things you can do to give yourself the best chance of getting enough of the right kind of sleep. Some of these might look like big lifestyle changes, but they are worth trying; after all, you can always go back to your old ways if the changes don't help.

▶ Don't eat a heavy meal just before bedtime – allow at least three hours for digestion.

▶ Avoid caffeine and alcohol in the evenings.

▶ Have a comfortable bed with a supportive mattress – use a board underneath if you can't afford a new mattress.

▶ Have the room dark enough for you – some people like pitch-blackness; others prefer a little light.

▶ Create a feeling of peace in the bedroom – no televisions or computers.

▶ Have the room warm or cool enough for you, and try to open the window during the day so that the air is fresh.

▶ Allow yourself to wind down gradually for at least half an hour before bed. Switch off your television and computer and have a peaceful routine for gradually closing down the household and ending your day.

- Do gentle yoga stretches before bed; this will relax your muscles.

- If you don't fall asleep after half an hour, or you are wide awake in the middle of the night, then get up for a little while. Go to another room and do something peaceful until you feel ready to sleep.

- Try not to nap during the day.

- Go to bed at the same time each night and get up at the same time each morning so that your body clock settles into a routine.

- However, if you feel you sleep too much as an escape, then gradually make your bedtime later and set the alarm earlier.

- Use a relaxation CD to help you wind down.

- Meditate regularly (but not at bedtime) – this will establish a habit of clearing your mind.

MINDFULNESS AND SLEEP

You can meditate during the evening, and it will help you clear your head of the day's events. However, it should also leave you feeling mentally alert, so don't do it too close to bedtime. Mindful breathing, on the other hand, can help you settle. If your mind is still whirling, focus on your breathing, gently bringing your mind back when it wanders.

Once you go to bed, don't focus desperately on getting to sleep. Mindfully observe yourself, and accept that sleep will come when your mind and body are ready. A body scan will help you seek out any physical tensions.

If you are sleeping too much, regular mindful meditation will help you accept rather than avoid those things that are troubling you. Alternatively, there are many CDs and downloads available with guided meditations for sleep. The simplest way to meditate for sleep, however, is to use the following variation of the relaxation exercise in Part one of this book.

Try it now: Get ready for sleep

Take your time going to bed and getting warm and comfortable. Lie on your back if possible, with your arms by your sides and your hands loosely relaxed. Allow your mind a moment to revisit the day and mentally say goodnight to everything that has happened during the day. If you find yourself thinking about worries and problems, tell yourself that it's OK to leave them for now and return to them in the morning.

Allow your breathing to slow down and become calmer. After a minute or so, scrunch your hands into fists, squeeze them tightly, then open out your fingers and relax your hands. Now work your way round your body tensing up various muscles, holding them for a moment and then relaxing. Start at your feet and work your way up. Don't forget the muscles in your face.

If you wish, you can now move into your normal sleeping position.

Now that your body is relaxed, you can allow your thoughts to drift. Create a natural scene in your mind that pleases you – either a real place or an imaginary one. Choose a garden, a beach, a riverside – whatever you like. This is your special place of safety, where you can relax and sleep. Spend as long as you wish there, enjoying the beauty and the solitude.

Focus points

1 Meditation often increases energy.
2 Tension burns up energy.
3 We're often too busy to listen.
4 Mindful listening helps you connect with people.
5 Reactions are automatic, responses are considered.
6 In a crisis, detach mindfully from your negative responses.
7 Practise mindfulness before crises arise.
8 Spend time in a natural environment.
9 Bring nature indoors.
10 Mindfully accept sleeplessness when it happens.

Next step

The next chapter will show you how a mindful attitude can help you deal with difficult experiences in everyday life.

16

Dealing with everyday difficulties

In this chapter you will learn:

▶ *how to use mindfulness to prepare for an exam or test*
▶ *how to cope with medical procedures mindfully*
▶ *about mindful travel.*

A mindful attitude can help you deal with experiences that you find difficult, tedious or unpleasant. Remember that the basis is always your regular mindfulness practice – it's no good suddenly deciding to be mindful the night before an exam or a dental appointment. When you're flustered, upset or nervous you won't be able to master an unfamiliar skill, so it needs to be already in place before you find yourself facing a difficulty. In any case, it's not sensible to suddenly change your ways just before, or in the middle of, a challenging life event. If you haven't taken time to familiarize yourself with meditation, you won't know how you will respond to it.

Exams and tests

Meditation before an exam or other type of test can be very helpful, calming nerves and helping you bring your full focus to the task in hand. Being fully in the moment is essential in an exam, and worries about the future (the results) and the past (not studying hard enough) are pointless and unhelpful. However, if meditation leaves you feeling very relaxed, then don't do it immediately before the exam. You'll learn from practice when is the ideal time for you to meditate before an exam.

Studying for an exam can be quite a tense process, made worse by the fact that sitting over a desk doesn't burn off any of the physical energy generated by tension. While studying, it is important to get up and walk around for a few minutes out of every hour, and you can combine the movement with mindful breathing. Pay particular attention to any part of your body that you know carries your tension.

During the exam itself, use moments of mindful breathing to anchor yourself in the present moment. If the exam has more than one part, take three mindful breaths between each part. You can ease your physical tension during the exam by stretching, or taking a permitted toilet break, using the opportunity to stand up and move around.

Medical procedures

Many of us dislike visiting the dentist, and the prospect of a surgical procedure, even a minor one, can cause anxiety. Meditating beforehand will help you go into the situation with calm acceptance. At the dentist, it may be possible to take an MP3 player with you and listen to a recording of a guided meditation while you are in the chair.

For many people, waiting is worse than the actual procedure, and again mindfulness can help you stay calm in the waiting room. In fact, it's an ideal place to practise, since you'll be safe, with nothing else to do but wait. Don't attempt a full meditation session in such a public place, and one where you also need to remain aware of your name being called or your number coming up. Instead, try a few minutes of mindful breathing or a mini body scan, focusing on those areas where you know you carry your impatience.

If you're the kind of person who starts to worry days before an appointment, then you'll find that your regular meditation sessions will help you keep a sense of perspective. This is not about trying to convince yourself not to worry, or that everything will be OK if there's a chance that it won't be. If you are facing something major, then mindfulness will help you to face it fully, while at the same time accepting and detaching from your own fearful emotions. If, on the other hand, you've become disproportionately worried about something comparatively minor, then mindfulness will help you accept that this has happened and there's no point in beating yourself up about it.

Key idea

Once you fully accept everything you're feeling, you're quite likely to find that the feelings become less intense.

Mindful travelling

Travel can be very stressful, and for many of us it's a question of persuading the time to pass as quickly as possible, since our real focus is on the destination. Mindful travelling is all about accepting that the journey is important in itself, and not something to be wished away.

We've already looked at mindful driving, but what about being a mindful car passenger? You can use journey times to meditate if you wish, although, if you suffer from motion sickness, start gradually with short sessions while you learn whether closing your eyes and surrendering to the motion of the vehicle is likely to upset you. There are alternatives to full meditation – a three-minute breathing space or a body scan can be done with your eyes open and fixed on the road ahead (which is also a very effective way of staving off motion sickness). If other people in the car are talkative, it's an ideal time to practise mindful listening.

If travel makes you tense, or you worry about arriving late or missing a connection, then use a three-minute breathing space to reground yourself, and a body scan to locate where you're carrying the tension and worry, so that you can breathe them away.

ROUTINE TRAVEL

Commuting to work, taking children to school and other journeys that we do regularly can soon start to feel tedious and irksome. You only have to look along any crowded commuter train to see how people feel the need to fill the time with Doing – working on laptops, reading newspapers or books, dealing with emails, making phone calls and so on.

For these routine journeys, you have different mindful options. You can devise ways to meditate, although you'll need to pay attention to your personal safety on public transport, and you certainly won't want to miss your stop. There will be many more distractions, of course, and once you are an experienced meditator you'll be able to use these as a challenge, something to observe but not engage with.

Another approach to a routine journey is to see it as an exercise in living in the moment. Behave as if it's the first time you're doing the journey, the first time you're seeing the sights, hearing the sounds, smelling the smells and feeling the movement. I regularly did a 30-minute drive to collect my children from school, but one day I was on the return route alone. Without the distraction of their chatter, I was able to notice that at one point there was a breathtaking view, and after that I was always aware of it.

Try it now: Travel mindfully

The next time you do a routine journey, decide to look at everything about the journey from a fresh perspective, as if it were your first time.

NEW JOURNEYS

If routine journeys can become tedious, new journeys can have almost too much uncertainty. Managing unfamiliar roads, stations and airports, delays, worrying whether you'll catch your connection, or whether your luggage is safe, finding places to eat and drink, remembering tickets and passports... all this can lead to sensory overload.

Forward planning is a great help of course, but you can't plan for the unexpected.

However the journey pans out, mindfulness will help you both cope with the difficulties and get the most out of the pleasures. The journey is part of the experience, not just a tedious and troubling interlude before you can resume your real life.

Here are some ways to restore calmness and clarity during an unfamiliar journey:

▶ Use mini meditations during delays or while waiting for connections.

▶ Take a three-minute breathing space if things start to get stressful.

▶ During long journeys, meditate for energy if you feel yourself flagging.

▶ Use a body scan to connect with any physical stress and breathe it away.

▶ Try to be fully present in every moment of the journey.

Focus points

1 Regular meditation gives you the basis for mindfulness.
2 Meditation will help stop worries building up before an event.
3 Work out the right time for you to meditate before an exam or test.
4 Use mindful breathing during an exam.
5 Take a mindful attitude to medical worries.
6 Use mindful breathing during medical procedures.
7 Travel mindfully on routine journeys.
8 Stay in the moment on unfamiliar journeys.
9 Meditate for energy on long journeys.
10 Use mini meditations during travel delays.

Next step

The next chapter will show you how to take exercise and do sport mindfully, even as a moving meditation.

17

Exercise and sport

In this chapter you will learn:

▶ *how to do mindful exercise*
▶ *about moving meditation*
▶ *about mindfulness and extreme sports.*

People who enjoy sport and physical activity will often describe how much they value the total engagement, which takes them for a short time away from their daily concerns into a place where nothing matters except what they are doing at that moment. Their internal chatter disappears and they only have to focus on one thing. They have found a kind of mindfulness, perhaps without realizing it.

Remember this

Any form of exercise can be undertaken mindfully, with full engagement in the experience of the exercise.

Many forms of exercise, such as running or going to the gym, can seem boringly repetitive and so there is a great temptation to listen to music or even, if you aren't too out of breath, make calls on your mobile phone. You put your body on autopilot to get on with the exercise while your mind engages with other things. However, this type of exercise can be turned into a moving meditation if you let go of all the distractions. Focus on your body, settle into the rhythm of the movement and allow your mind to empty of all thought.

Try it now: Exercise mindfully

The next time you exercise, try it without the headphones. If you have a companion, suggest that you maintain silence for this session. Allow yourself to focus fully on the exercise: the feelings in your muscles, the way your lungs work harder the more you exercise, the air on your skin, your contact with the ground, your bike, your boat or surfboard. Remember not to judge your performance or your fitness.

Case study

Like many people, I used to very much dislike exercise, and generally did it with the radio or MP3 player to keep me going. Exercising mindfully was a real challenge for me, but has turned out to be very rewarding because I am much more in tune with my body and I am, to my surprise, getting fitter.

Try it now: Do a moving meditation

Choose a repetitive activity and use it for a moving meditation. Before you start, make sure that you'll be safe while exercising and meditating. Focus on achieving a steady rhythm in the activity, and then use mindful breathing to take you into the meditation.

Non-competitive activities and exercise

As well as the need to be fit and burn calories, we undertake many physical activities for the pure pleasure they bring. Country walks, swimming in the sea and cycling down quiet lanes are all intensely pleasurable if undertaken mindfully.

If you exercise to improve fitness and burn calories, then meditation practice will help you work to your limits, accepting any breathlessness or muscular discomfort. Body scans will help you distinguish between discomfort that can be tolerated and body signals that mustn't be ignored. This means you'll be able to push your limits, increasing fitness and stamina, without damaging yourself.

Competitive sports

Competitive athletes are increasingly using mindfulness to help them in all aspects of their sport. This can seem contradictory, since a mindful attitude would seem to include accepting success or failure in competition, and detaching from the desire to win. On the other hand, if you are an intensely competitive person, then accepting that aspect of yourself is also mindful.

Athletes aim to be 'in the zone' – a state similar to flow (see Chapter 3) where you are totally in the moment, totally focused on your sport, and completely unaware of your internal chatter, time passing and even physical pain or fatigue.

Meditation before a sporting event can produce a calm, alert and focused state of mind. However, if your regular practice teaches you that after meditating you are actually too relaxed for physical exertion, then confine yourself to meditating the night before the event.

Mindfulness practice can help you with the four aspects of sport:

1 **Physical.** This is the training you do to be fit and strong, usually repetitive gym work. We've already seen that mindful awareness can help you stretch your limits while reducing the risk of injury.

2 **Technical.** This is the training you do to acquire the skills specific to your sport. Again, mindful awareness of your body will help you improve your skills. Being fully present in the moment will remove mental distractions and help you focus on improving your skills.

3 **Tactical.** This refers to your ability to make decisions in real time, as the match or race unfolds, or as you manage the terrain for something like skiing or white-water kayaking. The more fully present in the moment you are, the better your tactical skills will be and the greater your awareness of your surroundings and other people.

4 **Mental.** This is where mindful attention can make it far easier to get in the zone. The activity becomes effortless, you feel you have all the time in the world to react, your vision is enhanced, and in team sports you feel yourself to be totally unified with the rest of the team. You can let go of your analytical thinking mind and start to play your sport in ways that are entirely intuitive.

On the day of a sporting event, most athletes have a routine that brings them into the right state of mind. Fear of failure, anxiety about fitness, and worries about the quality of the other competitors can all be distractions that affect performance. You can adopt a mindful attitude, noticing these worries but not engaging with them, which will free you up to engage fully with the match or competition.

Extreme sports

Extreme sports can be both competitive (such as surf and climbing competitions) and non-competitive (surfing or climbing for the sheer thrill of it). However, for many practitioners the initial attraction is that the element of danger, which can be considerable, forces them into a state of mindful focus. Meditation before a difficult climb or before embarking on an epic surf session will help you be fully focused, calm and self-confident.

If you enjoy extreme sports, do you tend to think that the element of risk is what makes you feel fully alive, and that the rest of the time you are only half awake? Actually, it's the element of risk that forces you into a state of mindful awareness and *that* is what makes you feel fully alive. If you start a regular mindfulness practice, you'll gradually be able to extend that exciting, wide-awake feeling into your most mundane activities.

Focus points

1 You can achieve total mindful engagement in sport and exercise.
2 You can choose to do routine exercise mindfully.
3 You can meditate while doing any exercise with a rhythmic component.
4 Use body scan to improve your bodily sensitivity.
5 Mindfulness will help you work to your limits, accepting discomfort.
6 Mindfulness can help you be in the zone.
7 Mindfulness can help you with the four aspects of sport.
8 Meditate before an event to be fully alert and engaged.
9 Use mindfulness in extreme sports.
10 Bring the same level of engagement to daily activities.

Next step

The next chapter shows how we can use mindfulness to access our creativity and to help us overcome performance anxiety.

18

Enhancing creativity

In this chapter you will learn:

▶ *about mindfulness and creativity*
▶ *the relationship between Doing and Being and creativity*
▶ *how mindfulness can assist with performance anxiety.*

Some people are naturally and easily creative, but many of us find it difficult to access our creativity. We are inhibited by negative thoughts such as 'Oh, I can't draw' or 'I've got no imagination' and we gaze enviously at people who can conjure up a sketch or a story at the drop of a hat. We are often afraid of making mistakes, and afraid that other people will judge our creative work negatively.

I don't feel inhibited when I'm writing, but right now I'm trying to learn to dance and that's quite different. I have to let go of my belief that I'm too clumsy, and mindfully engage with the music and the steps of the dance.

Bear in mind that creativity isn't only about the traditional arts of painting, sculpture, music, drama, dance and literature. Craft activities are creative, as are cookery, organizing a room to make it more pleasing, or planting a garden with beautiful shapes and colours. Inventors are always creative thinkers. In fact, in its widest sense, creativity extends to everything we do.

Doing or Being?

Most people who enjoy being creative have to find ways to fit it into the rest of their life, and when they do finally get a moment to sit down at the keyboard or pick up a paintbrush, it can turn out to be very difficult to switch from one mode to another.

Creative activities seem to occupy a halfway house between Doing and Being and the creative person needs access to both. William Wordsworth tried to sum it up when he described the act of writing poetry as an expression of 'emotion recollected in tranquillity'.

Clearly, mindfulness practice will help you, first, to understand the difference between Doing and Being and, second, to move more easily between them. The more you meditate, the more you'll have access to Being mode and also the more you'll understand the transition between the two modes.

BEING IN THE MOMENT

Creativity is very much about responding with freshness and openness to the world around you. No one ever wrote a great poem or painted a great picture on autopilot. Artists in all disciplines talk about being transported while they're working, carried along by a flow of inspiration and energy. This is pure mindfulness, being fully present in the moment.

Aspects of creativity

In the 1970s the psychologist E. P. Torrance identified four aspects of creativity: fluency, originality, flexibility and elaboration.

FLUENCY

This is the process of generating ideas. There are various exercises that help access creativity, for instance:

▶ free thinking

▶ word association

▶ combining ideas

▶ finding new uses for everyday objects.

There are many more, but the one thing they all have in common is that you need to let go of judging the ideas you come up with and just let them flow. This is the first stage in the creative process – later on you can sift through the ideas and decide which are worth pursuing – but initially you need to sit back and observe the ideas as they pour out of your mind. Does this sound familiar? Yes, that's right, mindfulness also encourages you to observe rather than engage.

During meditation you encourage your mind to be still and empty, guiding it gently back if it darts off into thoughts, images and feelings. This may feel counter-intuitive for creativity, but in fact it opens your mind up so that you can work much more freely and openly when you return to your creative activity.

ORIGINALITY

Original ideas are different, new and often challenging. If you're going to have original ideas, you'll need to let go of conventional thinking and silence your inner critic. Regular meditation clears your mind of stale old thoughts and thought patterns, making room for new and original thinking.

FLEXIBILITY

Mental flexibility involves generating ideas across a broad range of possibilities and includes the ability to see things in different ways. One way to improve your creative flexibility is by asking questions:

▶ 'How would things look if the sky were red?'

▶ 'How does it sound if you play it backwards?'

▶ 'Supposing Prince Charming married one of the ugly stepsisters instead of Cinderella?'

▶ 'What can I use to paint with apart from a brush?'

A mindful habit of looking at the world openly and anew will help you come up with increasingly challenging questions and increasingly flexible answers to those questions.

ELABORATION

Once you have the ideas, you have to do something with them, and this is known as elaboration. At this point a creative person enters the space between Being and Doing, somehow managing to maintain both at the same time. Too far into Doing mode, and conventional judgement starts to creep in, thoughts start to run on tramlines and it's all too easy to slip into autopilot. Too far into Being mode, and there is no progress with the artwork.

The more you practise mindfulness, the more you will understand the two modes and the more you will be aware of where you are at any point in time.

Try it now: Be creative mindfully

Choose a creative activity and decide to engage with it mindfully. Your activity doesn't have to be artistic – it can be something like cooking or gardening.

Performance anxiety

Many people express their creativity through performance – playing an instrument, singing, acting, stand-up comedy – and many talented performers are held back by their performance anxiety (or stage fright). For some people it's a manageable tension that increases their alertness and reactivity on stage, but for others it's totally disabling.

Regular meditation practice will give you access to a calm inner space. Stage fright is fuelled by negative thoughts, but meditating beforehand will help you to let go of all thoughts. By meditating before a performance you'll be able to observe any rising panic without engaging with it, which will stop it spiralling out of control. Use a body scan to track any physical tensions, and breathe into them to release them.

PUBLIC SPEAKING

Every one of us at one time or another is likely to need to stand up and speak to a group of people, whether it's a speech at a wedding or a presentation at work or college. If this is something you do only rarely, it can seem very challenging. In fact, surveys have shown that public speaking is the number one dread, chosen by the greatest number of people as their greatest fear.

If you feel like this and yet you have to make a speech or give a presentation, then give yourself the best chance of success by rehearsing thoroughly and checking out the venue if it's an unfamiliar one.

Meditation will help you stay calm if you start to get nervous beforehand. Use a body scan to check out your physical tension, and allow yourself to breathe into it and release it. If you can detach yourself from your nervous feelings they are likely to quickly subside.

Focus points

1 Worrying about mistakes inhibits creativity.
2 Creativity extends to many activities.
3 Creativity needs both Doing and Being.
4 Creativity is in the moment.
5 Mindfulness can help you with the four aspects of creativity.
6 Too much anxiety can inhibit performance.
7 Negative thoughts drive stage fright.
8 Meditation can reduce performance anxiety.
9 Doing a body scan will help you release physical tension.
10 Detach from your nervous feelings.

Next step

The next chapter explains how to use mindfulness to foster healthy relationships – both with yourself and others.

19

Mindful relationships

In this chapter you will learn:

▶ *how to be honest about your relationship with yourself*
▶ *how to overcome negative self-talk*
▶ *about the importance of taking responsibility for your emotions*
▶ *how to change your expectations through mindful listening*
▶ *about the purpose of taking time out.*

Human beings are social animals and relationships are of key importance, whether it's the person you choose to live with for the rest of your life or the security person who greets you every day at work. Having healthy relationships with other people is one of the key factors in your sense of well-being and it has a huge impact on your levels of happiness.

Your relationship with yourself

If you aren't comfortable in your own skin, then what chance do you have of forming healthy relationships with other people? If you are a seething mass of resentments, jealousies and dissatisfaction, you'll project those on to other people and find it impossible to reach out to them in an open and warm way.

You already know that it isn't selfish to care for yourself (see Chapter 13), so start by looking at your relationship with yourself. Do you, in fact, like yourself? Do you find it too easy to beat yourself up over your failings and almost impossible to acknowledge your good qualities?

Try it now: Be honest about yourself

Make a list of your qualities. For every negative quality, include something positive. Don't judge or justify. Be as objective as possible.

Self-assessment

How did that feel? Did you find it hard to acknowledge your good qualities? Did you slip into comparing yourself with other people with thoughts like, 'I do try to be caring but I'll never be anything like my mum.' This exercise isn't about comparison or judgement. If you are caring, all you need to do is acknowledge that and put it on the list. Do the same with negative qualities: if you are, say, short-tempered, then write it down, and don't add 'but people are so annoying, aren't they?'

The chances are, first, that you find it difficult to acknowledge your good qualities. It's almost embarrassing, even though no one need ever see your list, and it feels like showing off. Second, you'll probably find it easier to admit to your negative qualities but at the same time you'll want to justify them. Let go of both of these behaviours, and do the exercise again.

Try it now: Be really honest about yourself

Make a list of your qualities. For every negative quality, include something positive. Don't be too embarrassed to list positive qualities, and don't justify negative qualities.

Self-assessment

Now that you have an honest list, keep it in your journal. The more you read it through, the more comfortable you'll feel with it. You may find that you change it and add to it over time.

Mindfulness and self-insight

Your regular meditation practice will give you greater insight into yourself, and will also start the process of acknowledgement and acceptance. (Remember, acceptance doesn't mean resignation. You accept how you are now, at this moment in time, but change is always possible.)

One thing you may become aware of is negative thinking, or 'negative self-talk' as it's often called. There are four main categories of negative self-talk, as seen in the following four sub-personalities:

▶ **The critic.** You tend to care what other people think about you, and assume that they're thinking something negative.

▶ **The victim.** You feel that the world's against you, and that you don't have any control over your life.

▶ **The worrier.** You always expect things to go wrong; you meet trouble halfway.

▶ **The perfectionist.** You feel that you'll never be good enough, and that you need to measure up to other people's expectations.

You may well recognize aspects of yourself in more than one of these categories, but probably one will dominate.

Self-assessment

Look at each of the four sub-personalities in turn and make notes about how each one relates to you. Take as long as you need to mull things over, but do decide which is your dominant sub-personality.

Try it now: Meditate to overcome negative self-talk

Start with mindful breathing. After a few minutes, open yourself to the concept of your dominant negative characteristic. Don't judge or criticize, or think about change. Simply accept that this is how you are, at this point in time. Take as long as you need for acceptance, and then move into loving-kindness mode. Extend a feeling of warmth and sympathy to yourself. Acknowledge that negativity is a form of suffering, and nurture yourself in a way that eases that suffering.

Self-assessment

How did that feel? When you identify your dominant sub-personality it is a huge step forward, but you probably still feel that somehow that negative voice in your ear is right about you, or that you deserve everything it says. When you extend the warmth of loving kindness to your negative sub-personality you're beginning to soothe and comfort yourself. Eventually you'll realize that it isn't your fault, and that you don't deserve to be unhappy.

Taking responsibility

The more you understand about yourself, the more you'll understand what it is you bring to relationships. Effectively, you'll take responsibility for your share in what goes wrong, or right. This is a very important step, because most of us have a tendency to say 'You always make me…'

'You always make me so cross.'

'You always make me unhappy.'

'You always make me flustered.'

'You always make me anxious' and so on.

We do much the same thing when things are going well:

'You make me so happy' and so on.

The truth is that we create our own emotions. When we think that other people have triggered an emotion, we are deluding ourselves and failing to take responsibility.

Imagine this scenario. You are due to meet up with an old friend but she doesn't turn up. You are worried and phone her mobile, sure that something has happened. It is only a car breakdown, and she was about to phone you, so all is well. But if it had been someone else rather than your friend, you might well have been angry rather than worried.

Imagine another scenario. You're at work, hurrying down the gangway between the desks, when you trip over an outstretched foot and wrench your ankle. Do you assume that someone stuck their foot out deliberately, or were they just sitting untidily? If the foot belongs to someone you dislike, do you immediately assume that they did do it deliberately? What about if they apologize, and explain that they had a bad back and were trying to find a way to sit comfortably? Are you mollified by this or do you refuse to believe it? Would you believe it if it was a friend? In each case, the pain from your wrenched ankle is the same, but your emotional response is different.

Remember this

You can always choose to be charitable and assume that people mean well, or you can assume that the world is against you and choose the knee-jerk reaction of anger.

Try it now: Take responsibility

Think about the last time you fell out with someone, or the last time you were irritated. How would it feel if you took full responsibility for the feelings you had at the time? Don't look for justifications – however provoking the other person was, however tired you were, simply accept that you created your feelings.

Adjusting your expectations

Part of what happens to us is due to our expectations. If you already have a problem getting on with someone, then you will tend to think they stuck their foot out intending to trip you up. Even just passing their desk, you might be braced for a sarcastic remark from them, ready to meet it with a riposte. Your expectations from friends are quite different and the warmth you feel for them leads you to tolerate behaviours that you'd never stand for from others.

When we make snap judgements about people, it's often because we have expectations based on past experiences. If your most-hated teacher at school was tall, thin and fair-haired, you might find yourself always having a negative reaction to anyone who looks a bit like that. Once you become aware of these things, you can take responsibility for them.

Try it now: Think about your expectations

Think about any difficult relationships that you have and work out whether your own assumptions and expectations could be part of the difficulty. Then set time aside for a loving-kindness meditation where you practise extending feelings of warmth and generosity to the people you struggle most to get on with. Don't expect to find this easy.

Mindful listening

We've already looked at mindful listening (see Chapter 15) and it is a key skill for mindful relationships. It starts with listening to yourself and understanding what it is that you need. Not listening to yourself can be another form of avoidance behaviour, a way of blocking off something painful. For instance, supposing you are always irritated by a neighbour who seems to have life totally organized, while yours is totally chaotic. When you glance out of the window and notice yet again their perfectly manicured garden, do you get a surge of guilt that you chose to watch television instead of working in your garden? And is that surge so painful that you turn it towards the neighbours, thinking to yourself crossly, 'Oh, they're such show-offs' or 'They're so anal – I'd hate to be like that.'

There may be deeper issues for you, too. Perhaps as a child you were often nagged for watching too much television, or you were forced to help in the garden and rather disliked it. So it's irritating when the neighbours tidy their garden and bring back these echoes of the past for you.

Mindfulness will help you understand why you do what you do in relationships. As the space between thought and action opens up, you'll find that there's room to look at where your knee-jerk reactions come from. Instead of blaming other people, you'll take responsibility, but also at the same time treat yourself gently and kindly. It's that attitude of kindness that will help you feel safe enough to face your own issues, and once you do that you'll be able to move on to looking at your other relationships.

Taking time out

We're used to the concept of time out for children; it takes them away from their unhealthy behaviour and gives them a chance to calm down and become more rational. In fact, time out is useful in all relationships when things get difficult, and mindfulness practice will help you to become aware of when you need time out and to make the most of it.

It's all too easy to get into a rut with relationships; we have the same old arguments over the same old issues. How often do we kick off with a regular 'You always…' at the start of a row? This is both failing to take responsibility and maintaining bad habits.

It helps to understand that when we're upset and angry we actually slip into 'fight or flight' mode (there is more on this primitive survival mechanism in Chapter 20). The physical and emotional changes that occur during fight or flight make it hard for us to empathize or see the other person's point of view. This made sense in the past – the human race wouldn't have got very far if people being chased by a wild animal were inclined to stop and think, 'Perhaps that man-eating sabre-toothed tiger is hungry, or has a cave full of baby tigers to feed, and I would make a decent meal for them.'

So the main function of time out is to help you come out of fight or flight mode and become more rational and empathic.

There are four stages to managing time out:

1 Discuss the use of time out with the person or people at a calm time. Explain that you won't be running away from the issue, but that you handle things better if you're allowed to calm down. Make it clear that you aren't trying to be controlling or avoiding the issue, but that everyone will benefit from the break.

2 When things start to get heated, and you're aware that you need to stop, then say clearly that is what you need to do.

3 Say how long you feel you need and make a commitment to return to the discussion at a specific time.

4 During the time out, do a three-minute breathing space. Allow yourself to calm down physically, and relax. Then examine the issue from a calmer perspective. Ask yourself why it is important to you, and try to understand why it's important to the other person or people. Let go of any desire to win, and aim for a solution that is right for everybody.

If you find yourself in a situation where you can't take a formal time out, then try to find a way to buy a little time for coming out of fight or flight mode. There's actually no shame in saying, 'Can you give me a moment; I just need to calm down a bit.'

Focus points

1 First, look at your relationship with yourself.
2 Acknowledge all your qualities.
3 Acceptance isn't resignation.
4 There are four main types of negative self-talk.
5 Take responsibility for your emotions.
6 Take responsibility for your behaviours.
7 Many problems arise from misplaced expectations.
8 Mindful listening is a key skill in relationships.
9 Learn to take time out when things get heated.
10 Don't use time out as a form of avoidance.

Next step

The next chapter explores feelings and emotions and how we can face them and detach from unpleasant ones instead of avoiding them.

20

Exploring feelings and emotions

In this chapter you will learn:

▶ *about the fight or flight response*
▶ *about our tendency to avoid or brood on emotions*
▶ *how to face emotions and detach from them.*

Remember this

If you have a diagnosed mental health problem, talk to your doctor or therapist before using mindfulness skills to explore your emotions.

For the next few chapters we'll look at aspects of your relationship with yourself, before looking more closely at your relationships with other people. As you already know, in Doing mode we tend to want to quickly put a stop to unpleasant emotions. We often mentally turn away from them and try to ignore not only the emotions but also the thoughts and body sensations that they bring with them. Part one looked at this briefly, and in this chapter we will go into it in greater detail.

The fight or flight response

The urge to get rid of unpleasant mental and physical sensations as quickly as possible comes from the primitive roots of Doing mode, which are connected with survival and the fight or flight mechanism. If an early human being was confronted with, say, a man-eating sabre-toothed tiger, he or she had two choices – fight back or run away. The huge surge of adrenalin that we experience when something terrifying happens is only part of a complicated mechanism that prepares us physically and mentally for this fight or flight. Both fight and flight require instant action, physical energy and totally focused thoughts.

Fear is an extremely uncomfortable sensation that can't be ignored, and the fight or flight mechanism is there to get us out of danger, and therefore away from fear, as quickly as possible. In Doing mode it is normal to take action to escape from unpleasant emotions and this is an important survival behaviour.

Avoiding emotions

The problems start when we make the easy mistake of allowing the Doing-mode response to affect how we manage all our emotions. Sadness, anger, jealousy and greed are all unpleasant in their own way, and Doing mode tells us to get rid of the unpleasantness as quickly as possible. So we try to turn our attention away from whatever we're feeling, and many of us try to make this even more effective by looking for an activity that brings us a quick fix of short-term happiness which distracts us from the unpleasant emotion.

Shopping, eating, watching television, alcohol and recreational drugs are common quick fixes. Not only are they capable of creating their own problems such as debt and addiction, but they simply don't work. The emotions are still there, smouldering away under the layers of avoidance and distraction. Imagine a bath full of water. If you leave the plug in, over time the water will become green and smelly. If you let the plug out, the water will run away. It's the same with your emotions – if you keep them in they fester, but if you let them out they will gradually disappear.

Try it now: Think about how you deal with unpleasant emotions

Spend some time thinking about how you deal with unpleasant emotions. Do you fight or run away? Do you try to soothe yourself with some masking activity or substance? Even in the privacy of your own thoughts, you might find it hard to be totally honest about this. If it helps, you can recall specific times when you felt unhappy or angry (or any other unpleasant emotions) and then recall what you did at the time by way of avoidance or masking. Don't try to make the emotions come fully to life – this exercise is not about actually experiencing them; it's about looking at your own behaviour.

Self-assessment

In your journal, make notes of the things you learned about yourself during this exercise. You may be able to add to the notes over time, as your insight into your own behaviours increases.

Rumination

As a writer with an active imagination, I find it all too easy to slip into ruminating. These days, as soon as I'm aware that I'm doing it, I take a three-minute breathing space to clear out my head.

Maybe you have a different type of reaction to difficult emotions – maybe you brood. Instead of turning away mentally, and looking for an external distraction, it may feel as if you are far too engaged with your emotions. For instance, when someone is rude to you on the phone, you may still be thinking about it days later, reliving the scenario, working out the clever things you could have said if only you'd thought of them in time, drafting letters to the company asking for the person to be sacked and so on.

Brooding, which is often known as rumination, is actually another kind of avoidance behaviour. Instead of feeling the emotional pain, you retreat into a kind of fantasy world, running the movie of the event in your mind and soothing yourself by making it happen differently or just by repeating it over and over. At the same time, of course, you are keeping the event open, like someone picking at a scab, and so this kind of avoidance can lead to very long-running low-grade misery.

Key idea

Rumination is a very clear-cut example of the 'second arrow of suffering' (see Chapter 14) and, if it becomes a habit, it can lead you to a negative world-view, in which everyone and everything is against you.

Positive emotions

As you can see, there are various ways of avoiding unpleasant emotions and trying to feel better quickly, but one thing that they all have in common is that they can lead to someone being cut off from all their emotions. Not letting yourself feel emotions or notice emotional signals becomes a habit, and this can include emotions that are positive and helpful, such as tenderness, tolerance and warmth.

In the rudeness on the phone scenario, the overwhelming urge to get away from the pain might stop you having more charitable thoughts, such as:

'Perhaps the person was having a bad day.'

'Perhaps they misheard me.'

'Perhaps I misheard them.'

'Perhaps it doesn't matter that much anyway.'

In this scenario, the person at the other end of the phone is anonymous and you'd probably never come across them again. However, if you extend emotional avoidance into all your relationships, you could find yourself losing sight of all your positive emotions. Not only is this disastrous for the relationships, but it will lead you to be unhappy and dissatisfied with your life.

Mindful detachment

I had a phone call telling me my adult son was ill on the other side of the world. My overwhelming instinct was to 'do something', but I couldn't possibly be there in time to help as he needed emergency surgery. All I could do was accept what I was feeling, and try to be detached from the feelings.

If you use mindfulness skills, you can both face your emotions and detach from them. During your regular meditation sessions you'll learn that sometimes emotions do rise up, and if you allow them to do so, with both acceptance and gentle curiosity, then you won't be overwhelmed.

As you become more secure in your practice, you can let yourself face the more challenging emotions in your life while meditating, and by doing this you're likely to reduce their impact. In other words, some emotions are a bit like the monster that a child sees in the corner of the dark bedroom – turn on the light and it turns out to be just a pile of toys.

Mindful detachment allows you to observe your emotions without engaging with them. Try not to judge yourself while you're observing. Thoughts such as 'Here I go again, losing it over nothing' or 'It never goes right for me' are part of the unhelpful habits that people develop for managing their emotions. Observe, be interested, and be as kind to yourself as you would to a small distressed child. This is quite different from avoiding emotions or masking them – you acknowledge, accept and face them, but you also let go and detach from them.

If you find that you have emotions welling up from a deep source, perhaps from far in the past, then you can use mindfulness skills to face, observe and detach from them.

Remember this

Don't discount the idea of turning to a therapist or counsellor – mindfulness isn't the only way to deal with difficulties, and if you need help from another source, that's fine.

Changing unhelpful habits

The raft of unhelpful habits that many of us develop in our emotional lives can be very difficult to change. The brain's limbic system is responsible for our emotions, and this appears to be a very primitive part of the brain that developed in response to the pressures of trying to survive in a hostile world. It cuts in fast, as soon as we feel under pressure, and is very powerful. Changing brain function can be a challenge, but brain scans are showing us more and more that the brain does change if we change our behaviours.

As we've already seen in Chapter 5, repetition is the key. The more you do something, the more the pathways in your brain develop, and so the more easily you are able to do it. This is why our avoidance behaviours get such a grip on us – the more we do them, the more comfortable they feel, and the more they tend to happen on autopilot. Because of this, mindful detachment will seem difficult at first, when you're swept up in the emotion of the moment, or when you're focused on running away from the emotion, but each time you make the effort to detach you will manage it a little, and that will make it easier for the next time.

All emotions are short-lived, and the idea of making changes is not to bring you to a state where you are continuously happy and joyful. That wouldn't be realistic. It's more that, if you are able to accept your painful emotions, face them and be fully present with them, then you'll find you're more able to experience your positive emotions and get the full benefit from them for as long as they last. In other words, your emotions will be in balance.

Key idea

All emotions are transient, and if we use mindfulness to observe and accept our negative emotions, knowing that they will pass, we will be more able to experience the positive ones.

Try it now: Stay with your emotions

At your next meditation session, focus on your emotions. Start, as usual, with mindful breathing. As you breathe, mentally release the barriers around your emotions so that you're able to feel them. Allow yourself to observe them, accept that they exist, and watch as they pass over you. Be kind to yourself, and don't judge yourself if the emotions are ones you'd rather not have, such as jealousy or resentment. If you stay detached, then they, too, will pass.

Focus points

1 Fight or flight is a primitive survival mechanism.
2 It's natural to want to avoid fear.
3 Avoiding emotions isn't helpful for relationships.
4 Quick-fix behaviours are often unhelpful.
5 Brooding is part of avoidance.
6 You can end up cut off from your positive emotions.
7 Mindful detachment allows you to observe your emotions without engaging.
8 Change can be difficult.
9 Change your behaviour and you can change your brain.
10 Emotions are short-lived.

Next step

The next chapter discusses how mindfulness can improve our mental health.

21

Mindfulness and mental health

In this chapter you will learn:

▶ *that you can improve your mental health through mindfulness*
▶ *to assess your own unhealthy habits*
▶ *how to go about making changes.*

It's easy to feel that 'I am what I am' and that we don't have any power to change ourselves. It can also be quite scary to think that we can make changes to aspects of ourselves that feel so solid and permanent. Most of us find it easier to accommodate our quirks and even justify them – 'I'm silly sometimes but at least I'm fun,' or 'I'm hopeless with money, but at least I'm not mean.'

It's true that you can't escape from yourself – whatever you do, wherever you go, you'll always take yourself along with you – and it's also true that you might as well learn to live with yourself. However, there are healthy and unhealthy ways of doing this.

Improving mental health

It's generally thought that mentally healthy people have somehow acquired an internal mental gyroscope that keeps them balanced. It's like having a good parent always inside you, guiding you through life. (I was lucky enough to have caring parents, but the voice I hear when I need guidance and support is my granny's.) It helps if your real parents were wise and caring, but some people find their own way to create this inner parent even after a poor childhood experience. Mentally healthy people don't need other people to like them, or for life to be perfect, before they can be happy. Mindfulness offers you a way to create your own internal good parent.

Try it now: Care for yourself

Give yourself the gift of a loving-kindness meditation that's entirely for you. Start, as usual, with mindful breathing. Take your attention to your diaphragm and imagine that every time you breath in, a warm glow of kindness spreads from your middle into your entire body. Now think about your good qualities. It might help to use the words 'I'm lovable because...' Give yourself full credit for the kind acts you do, your desire to do well and your caring nature. You don't have to be reticent; remember, no one is listening in. Then move on to the qualities you're less pleased with. Face them, and forgive yourself.

We've already seen that many of us use more or less unhealthy habits to avoid the pain of unpleasant emotions, and that we often pay the price of both the consequences of the habits and of being cut off from our pleasant emotions. Surely it's worth making changes in order to improve matters? Can you imagine a life free of the restrictions imposed by your self? Instead of making endless resolutions that you'll never keep (save more, lose weight, stay calm, get fit and so on), why not make the changes that will lead to you living in a better, healthier way?

Research has shown that there is quite a lot we can do to improve our mental health. We all have basic human qualities, such as the fight or flight mechanism. We all have a certain genetic make-up. We were all affected and moulded in childhood by our parents and the people around us (family, school friends and so on). None of these things can be changed, although we can learn to manage them. What's more, all of those things put together add up to only 60 per cent of who we are. This means that there is 40 per cent that is within our power to change.

Try it now: Understand yourself

Spend some time thinking about your childhood and look at how your current attitudes and beliefs were shaped by it. Most experiences have both positive and negative impact – try to see both. Don't expect to see the full picture the first time you do this exercise, but be prepared to return to it from time to time.

Self-assessment

Keep a record in your journal of your thoughts from the exercise above, and add to it as new insights occur to you.

Other things that have been shown to help improve mental health are:

▶ keeping an active mind by taking on new learning challenges

▶ regular physical exercise

▶ self-awareness

▶ embracing change rather than resisting it.

Looking at change

You can't make changes until you know what it is that needs changing. That may sound blindingly obvious, but you only have to look at other people to see that very often they keep blundering through life without understanding why they're unhappy, or why they keep making the same mistakes. The chances are that you and I are no different; it's just much harder to look at yourself in the same objective way. The exercise you've just done will help you work out what it is that you need to change.

The next step is to face the need to give up your 'comfort blanket'. This can be pretty tough. It doesn't matter if yours is something clearly harmful – such as smoking – or something less obviously so – such as retreating into the fantasy world of online gaming – if it is your way of avoiding your emotions, you will need to give it up. In the previous chapter you began to identify your personal comfort blankets, and you also began the process of detaching from the emotions that you've tended to avoid.

One of the reasons we keep habits going, even when they aren't very helpful, is that it's the path of least resistance, something we can do on autopilot. You already know that coming out of autopilot takes some effort, but you also already know that there are rewards when you do so. Being fully present in the moment is truly living your life rather than coasting through it.

Key idea

Making changes can be difficult but, as counsellors often say to their clients: 'If you do what you've always done, then you'll get what you've always got.'

Case study

My mother tried for years to give up smoking, without success. She knew what needed changing, but it wasn't till her first bout of bronchitis that she faced the need to let go of the comfort smoking gave her. Once she was able to truly face what she was doing, she realized at once that, unlike many smokers, she actually smoked the most when she was alone. She rearranged her schedule to include much more socializing, and finally managed to give up smoking.

Making changes

As well as your regular meditation sessions, you can use mindfulness at times when you feel the need to turn to your comfort blanket. Use a short body scan to focus on the places where you feel the restless desire to avoid an emotion. Also, use a three-minute breathing space to put some distance between yourself and the desire. In fact, changing any habitual behaviour can start with creating a little space between the desire and the action. You may still, after the three minutes, have a cigarette or turn on the television, but that three minutes is the beginning of teaching your mind that it can do without.

Try it now: Breathe mindfully and smile

You already know that changing your body language can change your mood, so it's likely that deliberately smiling will cheer you up. Take a few mindful breaths and then smile, quietly and gently. Don't worry if you're not that cheerful inside – give the smile a chance.

Focus points

1 You can't escape from yourself.
2 You can make changes.
3 You can create an internal 'good parent'.
4 Accept all your qualities.
5 Be kind to yourself.
6 You can improve your mental health.
7 You need to know what it is that needs changing.
8 Keeping on with old habits is the easy option.
9 You may need to give up your comfort blanket.
10 Remember to smile.

Next step

The next chapter explains the difference between good and bad stress and how mindfulness can help you manage your stress response.

22

Mindfulness and stress

In this chapter you will learn:

▶ *the difference between good and bad stress*
▶ *how to assess your stress*
▶ *about managing stress.*

Remember this

If you have a diagnosed mental health problem, talk to your doctor or therapist before using mindfulness skills to manage stress.

Good stress and bad stress

We all worry about stress these days, without really distinguishing between good stress and bad stress. A certain amount of stress gives us energy and focus, and without it life would be boring and without challenge.

Think of all those affluent Victorian women, with nothing to do and nothing to worry about, and think how many of them became chronic invalids. The writer Elizabeth Barrett was thought to be so fragile that she had to live in a gloomy, airtight room and have very few visitors. Yet when she escaped to a life in Italy and marriage (to Robert Browning), she was able to walk for miles, cope with the stress of money worries and several miscarriages, and with raising the one child she did have. She needed a little stress in her life to make it worth while.

Key idea

As we saw in Part one, you need a little stress to find 'the zone' and be happy. If you remember, to have flow you need to be 'feeling competent, and that the task is a challenge but within your abilities'.

Good stress is short-lived and doesn't overwhelm you. It's part of what makes you feel alive and connected with the world around you. However, periods of recovery between stressful events are essential, so that the fight or flight mechanism can close down and your systems can return to a relaxed state. During these non-stressed periods, your body automatically replaces any resources that have been used up, and your mind recovers its equilibrium.

Bad stress, on the other hand, is long-term and relentless. It overwhelms and exhausts you, and can have disastrous effects on your physical and mental health. You use up resources faster than you can replenish them, and your fight or flight response may become permanently switched on.

Each one of us reacts differently to bad stress, but the possibilities include irritability, poor sleep, raised blood pressure, anxiety, depression and flare-ups of chronic illnesses such as eczema. Stress can affect your body, your behaviour, your emotions and your thoughts.

Measuring your stress

We all vary in how well we cope with long-term stress. Some people have calm natures, or find it comparatively easy to keep a sense of proportion. Others are more easily upset and get easily stressed. Whatever you're like, there's no point in beating yourself up about it. Remember, the mindful approach is to accept yourself as you are, without judging.

Despite the huge variations between people, research has showed that certain key life events are stressful for most people. If too many of these come along close together, then you are likely to become stressed. This is because there isn't time between each stressful event for your system to return to normal and for your resources to be replenished.

Try it now: Measure your stress

The table below shows the Holmes-Rahe Stress Scale, devised in the 1960s as a way of measuring stress. The idea is to look at your life over the last two years and add up the scores for any of the events you've experienced.

Life event	Score
Death of a spouse	100
Divorce	73
Marital separation	65
Imprisonment	63
Death of close relative	63
Personal injury/illness	53
Marriage	50
Dismissal from work	47

Marital reconciliation	45
Retirement	45
Change in health of relative	44
Pregnancy	40
Sexual difficulties	39
New family member	39
Business readjustment	39
Financial change	38
Change in marital rows	35
Major mortgage	32
Foreclosure of mortgage/loan	30
Work responsibilities change	29
Child leaves home	29
Trouble with in-laws	29
Big personal achievement	28
Spouse starts/stops work	26
Start/stop school	26
Living conditions change	24
Personal habits change	24
Trouble with boss	23
Work hours/conditions change	20
Moving house	20
Change school	19
Change recreation	19
Alter church activities	19
Alter social activities	18
Small mortgage/loan	17
Alter sleeping habits	16
Change in family reunions	15
Alter eating habits	15
Holidays	13
Christmas	12
Minor law breaking	11

Self-assessment

If you score more than 150 points then you are likely to be stressed, and the more points you have above 150 the more chance there is of you becoming ill, either physically or mentally. Use your journal to record the results of this assessment.

You'll have noticed that even enjoyable events, such as getting married, holidays and Christmas, are stressful. Also, the scale doesn't make much allowance for how long the stressor lasts. 'Change in health of a relative' scores 44 points – and even if they recover quickly, you will be stressed. However, if the illness is serious and long term, your stress is likely to become chronic.

The Holmes-Rahe Scale helps you identify where some of your stress might be coming from. However, if you have a low score and yet you still feel stressed it may be simply that your life has unusual stress factors in it. Also, the scale doesn't allow for ongoing factors such as a difficult daily commute that you might have been doing for years, or a constant work overload. So another way to measure your stress is with self-assessment via a questionnaire.

Self-assessment: How stressed am I?

How many of the following statements do you agree with? If something happens only very occasionally, answer no; answer yes for things that occur frequently.

1 I often forget to eat well.

2 I often forget to exercise.

3 I often forget to relax.

4 I often have a dry mouth, shallow breathing, the shakes or excessive sweating.

5 I often think I have to do everything.

6 I often lose my cool.

7 I often try to do too much.

8 I often miss the joke.

9 Everything is a big deal to me.

10 I often feel I'm disorganized.

11 I often forget to share my worries.

12 I often feel I'm alone with it all.

13 I often keep putting things off.

14 I often think I've had a raw deal.

15 I often have to go at top speed.

16 My way is the only way.

17 I often feel overwhelmed.

18 I often feel that nothing has much point.

19 I often ignore my stress symptoms.

If you agreed with eight or more of the statements, then you're stressed, even if you can't identify the causes, and the more yes answers you gave, the more stressed you are. Use your journal to record the results of this assessment.

Responses to stress

There are helpful and unhelpful ways of responding to stress, and even if your responses are actually unhelpful they will still seem to you to be the most easy and comfortable. They may be something you learned as a child, or habits you've slipped into over the years. Examples of unhelpful responses are:

▶ overeating

▶ not eating enough

▶ too much caffeine

▶ too much alcohol

- ▶ negative thinking
- ▶ not making time for friends and family.

Examples of more helpful responses are:

- ▶ taking regular short breaks
- ▶ exercising
- ▶ socializing
- ▶ enjoying music, theatre and cinema
- ▶ meditating.

Try it now: Look at your physical stress response

Take the time to think about how stress affects you. Do you let it out by getting angry easily, or do you hold it in and use quick fixes like alcohol to cope? Where do you feel it in your body? Do you get tension headaches, or irritable bowels, or something else?

Self-assessment

Use your journal to record the results of this exercise. The next time you are feeling stressed, do a body scan and check out your whole body. This will also help you find out where you carry your stress.

When you're stressed your body responds with the same fight or flight mechanism that we looked at in Chapter 20. As we have seen, this is designed to be short-lived – a quick burst of energy to get you out of trouble, followed by the relaxation response, which returns your body to normal once the danger is over. You now know that if you're experiencing long-term stress you may be permanently in fight or flight mode, which, if you think about it, inevitably uses up your resources faster than you can replenish them. You may reach a point where you're permanently wired and unable to switch off the stress response.

WHAT TRIGGERS THE STRESS RESPONSE

It may seem to you as if your stress response is instantaneous and automatic, but in fact it all starts with a thought. Unless your thinking mind decides that a situation is stressful, you won't have a physical stress response. The triggering thought is usually that you can't cope with what's being thrown at you. If you think about it, it makes sense. Someone who is in the zone, doing something that they feel competent to do, will experience flow. As soon as they think that they can't cope, there is no more flow, only worry and stress.

Imagine a situation where a dog runs at you barking. If it's your dog and you know that's how he greets you, you won't be afraid and you won't experience a stress response. If he's an unknown dog, you'll be likely to interpret the barking and movement as aggression. You'll feel afraid and experience a stress response. In both cases, it's your thinking mind that is in charge.

LIVING ON AUTOPILOT

If you are in permanent fight or flight mode, you are probably also on permanent autopilot. Rushing from crisis to crisis with no time to stop and think, constantly juggling and multi-tasking, is a fairly typical twenty-first-century stress pattern.

The mental side of stress is very much about feeling out of control. We talk about things being too much, of things getting on top of us. On autopilot, we may well be living in the moment, but without mindful awareness we are rushed along far too fast – the autopilot is in charge. Mindfulness can help you turn off the autopilot, become more aware of what's happening and feel more in control.

Key idea

If you've read this far in the book and started a mindfulness programme, congratulations! Just by doing that, you're taking a step back from your stress.

Stress and other people

One side effect of long-term stress and being on permanent autopilot is that you tend to forget about other people and the fact that they can potentially support you. It's as if you're in a tunnel, rushing ever forwards and never looking anywhere else but straight ahead at the next challenge, and all the other challenges lined up behind it. I realized too late that I could have helped a friend through a difficult patch. When I queried why he hadn't asked for help, he said, 'I never thought of it; I had my head down getting on with things.' He was on autopilot, and forgot all about his friends.

There are two ways in which you can reach out to other people for their help in times of stress:

1 **Maintain your social contacts.**

   Keeping up with friends and family is a healthy way to rebalance yourself and regain perspective.

2 **Ask for help.**

   Remembering to ask for help from colleagues will actually change your workload. This is true both at work and at home – you may need to discuss with your partner how you organize the chores and other commitments as well as looking at how your working day is organized.

Try it now: Meditate on other people

Do a loving-kindness meditation focusing on the people close to you, both at work and at home. Let go of any resentments you feel about their failure to help, and instead think of them with warmth and friendliness. Remind yourself that they can't help you if they're unaware that there's a problem.

Some stress is self-created. If you've got locked into Doing mode, it's easy to think that you're the only one who can do everything and no one else can be relied on. Not only is this a lonely position to be in, but just think for a moment what you take away from other people by not giving them the chance to take on responsibility.

Case study

I knew a teacher who was the only one not to organize a stall at the school fête for his group of 14-year-olds. I thought he was being lazy but when I challenged him he pointed at a stall and said, 'Look, they got so fed up waiting for me to do it they went ahead and arranged it on their own. How much do you think they learned about teamwork and organization from doing that compared with if I'd done it?'

Mindful ways to manage stress

Regular meditation is the key part of a mindful stress-management programme. If you see mindfulness as a quick-fix technique to be called on only when you need it, then it's unlikely to help, although you may achieve a moment of calm from mindful breathing or a short body scan. However, if you start each day with a mindful meditation rather than feeling you have to hit the ground running, then you'll be far more likely to cope with whatever the day throws at you. And the effects are cumulative so, as the days pass, your levels of bad stress will go down.

Regular meditation, then, is the foundation, and on top of that you can place mini meditations, short body scans to relax any tense muscles and three-minute breathing spaces at strategic moments during the day. Also, practise mindfully carrying out some of the activities that cause you stress – once a day perhaps, deliberately focus on doing something mindfully that you would normally find stressful. The more you do this, the more you will learn to focus on the task and let go of any stress.

In addition, remember to take proper breaks, with fresh air if possible (such as a short walk in your lunch hour), include time for leisure activities and remember to stay connected to other people. All of these will help you maintain a good perspective on the things that are causing you stress, which in turn will help you prioritize what really needs to be done and what you can actually let go of.

Remember this

As you become more aware of your body and the workings of your own mind, use mindful breathing whenever you become aware of your particular stress response building up.

Mindfulness-based stress reduction (MBSR)

Stress reduction was one of the first uses of mindfulness in the Western world, via a course devised by Jon Kabat-Zinn. He created the eight-week model (see Chapter 12) and thousands of people have benefited from the course. The courses are run in a group setting, which has the benefit that you meet other people with stress-related problems, share your experiences and support one another as you all explore mindfulness. Use the Internet to find out whether there's a course near you.

Focus points

1 Not all stress is bad for you.
2 You can assess your own stress levels.
3 Even happy events create some stress.
4 Some responses to stress are damaging or unhelpful.
5 With enough stress, your fight or flight mode can be permanently 'On'.
6 Stress starts with a thought.
7 You can feel out of control when stressed.
8 Stress can make you feel lonely.
9 Social activities help reduce stress.
10 Use mindfulness to manage stress.

Next step

In the next chapter you'll learn about the thought processes that lead to us becoming angry and how to manage our anger with a mindful approach.

Mindfulness and anger

In this chapter you will learn:

▶ *about the reasons for anger*
▶ *about the physical signs of anger*
▶ *about the thoughts that trigger anger*
▶ *how to manage anger.*

Remember this

If you have a diagnosed mental health problem, talk to your doctor or therapist before using mindfulness skills to deal with anger.

Getting angry is all part of our primitive survival mechanism. Anger is there to arouse us so that we protect ourselves and our defenceless children from attack. Anger is therefore one of a range of possible responses to a physical threat. Inevitably, we find ourselves responding with anger to other kinds of threat, too, but in the modern world it can be quite inappropriate to do so.

Try it now: Study anger

It's much easier to understand what goes wrong for other people than for ourselves. Think back to times when you've seen someone get angry or irritated and try to work out what triggered their anger. Obviously, something happened to set them off, but can you see *why* that person reacted with anger? Choose situations where you weren't the focus of the anger, but a witness to it, so that your memories aren't coloured by your own emotions.

Often, it's quite easy to see what's going on for other people – you can see that they're tired and stressed, or they feel they're being shown up in public, or they have over-high expectations of another person or organization. No doubt you'll realize at once that in most cases the perceived threat either didn't exist or wasn't severe enough to warrant anger. We see people get angry if a waiter brings cold food, if a queue moves too slowly or if someone cuts them up on the road. If you happened to know the angry person quite well, you might also realize that their anger says more about them and how they see the world than it does about the situation that provoked the anger.

Self-assessment

Think back to the last time you were angry. Try to work out why your anger was triggered. Something happened, but why did you get angry? Were you tired and stressed, standing on your dignity, or did you have over-high expectations? Be honest with yourself and make notes in your journal about the sources of your anger.

Physical signs of anger

Anger creates uncomfortable physical sensations, and expressing our anger is partly a way of trying to make the sensations go away. They might include:

- tight or churning stomach
- clenched fists
- clenched jaw
- shoulders raised and tense
- sweating
- pounding heart
- fast breathing
- shaking.

Self-assessment

Think about your own anger, and work out how what sensations it produces in your body. Then make notes in your journal about how you feel your anger physically.

Triggering thoughts

You may not be aware of it, but there are thought processes that lead to anger, and these vary from person to person depending on their core beliefs about the world. If you have a chip on your shoulder, you'll be likely to get angry if you think someone is talking down to you. If, on the other hand, you think everyone is out to con you, then you'll be likely to overreact angrily to something like being given the wrong change. The trouble is that the thoughts happen so quickly that mostly we aren't aware of them, and we assume that our anger is an inevitable gut reaction with no input from our thinking minds.

Here are some examples of thoughts that might flash through your mind just before you get angry:

- ▶ 'Who does he think he is?'

- ▶ 'I'm not standing for this.'

- ▶ 'How dare they treat me like this?'

- ▶ 'I've stood enough of this.'

- ▶ 'I never get any respect.'

- ▶ 'You always treat me like this.'

- ▶ 'You always make me angry.'

In these thoughts you can see a mixture of standing on your dignity (How *dare* they...), over-generalizing (You *always*...) and blaming other people for your anger (You always *make me*...).

Self-assessment

Think about your own anger, and try to work out what your thought processes are just before you get angry. Make notes in your journal about the thoughts you have.

The mindful approach to anger

One definition of mindfulness is that it takes place in the gap between thought and action. The more you practise meditation, the bigger that gap becomes and the easier you'll find it to remember to be mindful at difficult times. Once you understand your own thought processes, you'll be on the lookout for them. Also, once you've identified them and examined them rationally, you'll see that they don't make a lot of sense.

Loving-kindness meditation offers you the chance to explore more positive options. The more often you do this meditation, the more you'll be able to enlarge your kindly feelings to embrace even those people and situations that make you angry.

Using this as a basis, you can also learn to be mindful at the moment when anger arises. You can let go of the physical sensations by breathing and gently releasing tension. Breathe in calmness, and breathe out your tension. Try not to turn away from the uncomfortable sensations; by staying with them you'll allow them to wash over you and dissipate more quickly. If the physical discomfort threatens to become unbearable, try stretching to release the tension in your muscles or walking about gently, reconnecting with the ground or floor beneath you.

Observe your thoughts, and notice whether you're slipping into your particular angry thinking pattern. Detach yourself from your thoughts, accept that they're there but also accept that you don't have to act on them.

Once the anger has passed, treat yourself gently for a while. Try to reconnect with your senses, and seek out something calming – maybe gaze up at the sky while your mind settles. Don't judge yourself too harshly – like everyone, you are a work in progress. You can also make good use of the energy that anger creates, either by taking some exercise or by getting on with something that needs doing.

Case study

I opened the cupboard, and everything fell out. I felt angry with the rest of the family, who'd stuffed things in any old how, but I was alone in the house. So, instead of ranting and raving, I used that energy to clear out the cupboard, throwing a lot of rubbish away and putting the rest back tidily.

Focus points

1 Anger is part of survival.
2 We each have our own anger triggers.
3 Anger produces strong physical sensations.
4 It's natural to want to get rid of anger.
5 Anger is triggered by thoughts.
6 Core beliefs underlie anger triggers.
7 You can work out your own triggers.
8 Mindfulness will help you detach from anger.
9 Extend loving-kindness to the people who make you angry.
10 Be kind to yourself once the anger has passed.

Next step

The next chapter will help you assess your anxiety and how it affects you. It also describes anxiety disorders, panic attacks and OCD and how to cope with them using a mindful approach.

24

Mindfulness and anxiety

In this chapter you will learn:

▶ *to assess your anxiety and how it affects you*

▶ *how to develop a mindful approach to anxiety*

▶ *about anxiety disorders, including panic attacks and OCD, and how mindfulness can help.*

Remember this

If you have a diagnosed mental health problem, talk to your doctor or therapist before using mindfulness skills.

A certain amount of anxiety is normal and healthy. It helps us to be aware of danger, and it is part of the way we learn from experience. Imagine a person with no sense of danger trying to cross a busy road and you'll see why anxiety is part of our make-up.

Self-assessment: How anxious am I?

Here is a test to help you assess your anxiety. Do the stress self-assessment in Chapter 22 first. See how many of the statements you agree with, and only answer yes if it happens frequently.

1 I often find it difficult to relax.

2 I often feel dissatisfied with my life.

3 I often feel edgy.

4 I often spend time analysing myself.

5 I worry about losing control.

6 I never get on top of my to-do list.

7 If I have a problem, I can't stop thinking about it.

8 Everyone else seems happier than me.

9 I'm easily upset.

10 I often feel I can't breathe, or that there's a lump in my throat.

11 I'm often sweaty, or cold and clammy.

12 I can often feel my heart pounding.

13 I'm afraid of the future.

If you agreed with more than six of the statements, then you have a high level of anxiety. The more yes answers you have, the more anxious you are. You may also see a correlation between your stress levels and your anxiety levels. Use your journal to record the results of this assessment.

Anxiety is triggered by the same fight or flight response as stress, and that is why someone with long-term stress can often also experience high levels of anxiety. We each have our own level of tolerance of stress and our own response to it, so that some people will become anxious very easily and others will remain calm even though they're under pressure. If you easily become anxious, don't waste energy beating yourself up about this. Mindfully observe yourself, and remind yourself that change starts with acceptance of how things are.

Anxiety is another mental state that did not evolve for long-term use. It's part of being aware of and dealing with threats, but when the danger has passed the anxiety should subside and your mind and body should return to a relaxed state. If you've been under a lot of pressure over a period of time, you may have lost the ability to relax, and as a result you may be permanently anxious.

Anxiety is very uncomfortable, both physically and mentally, so our initial reaction as soon as we start to feel anxious is to try to get rid of it. It's often a classic case of a knee-jerk reaction rather than a considered response. For instance, if your teenage son or daughter is a few minutes late home, you start to feel worried about them, so you pick up the telephone and dial their mobile to find out why. No harm done perhaps, except that the teenager feels hassled and you have reinforced your habit of giving in to anxiety. A considered response might be to check the bus timetable, or wait a little longer and then send a text rather than phone.

Key idea

If your background level of anxiety is always high, then small events are likely to trigger an unreasonably big anxiety reaction. You might also expect anxiety to affect you physically in the same way as stress (see Chapter 22), but it isn't always the case. For example, I feel pure stress in my stomach, but anxiety lodges itself in my head.

The mindful approach to anxiety

Research has shown that the brains of people who practise mindful meditation have fewer active fear centres than the brains of those who don't meditate, so maintaining your regular programme is the basic way to approach reducing your background anxiety. (Background anxiety is the anxiety you feel all the time if you are in permanent fight or flight mode.)

If you feel anxious, and are about to carry out a knee-jerk reaction, it's always worth taking a few mindful breaths and asking yourself, 'Is my reaction reasonable or am I just trying to get rid of my anxiety?' Remember that we instinctively try to avoid unpleasant emotions, but the mindful way is to accept and face them. You can learn to accept that you're feeling anxious, that there is a reason for it, that it is painful, and that some pain is inevitable in life.

Anxiety disorders

If you experience continual feelings of anxiety and worry, it may in fact be your way of avoiding and masking even deeper emotions. This is often the case for people whose anxiety becomes so chronic that they develop an anxiety disorder. These can range from mild to severely disabling and they include panic, agoraphobia, social phobia and obsessive-compulsive disorder (OCD). Although anxiety disorders have widely varying symptoms, they are all driven by overwhelming anxiety that leads to various kinds of avoidance behaviours and compulsions.

Remember this

Don't try to self-diagnose an anxiety disorder – talk to your doctor.

For a long time now, cognitive behaviour therapy (CBT) has been the preferred treatment for anxiety disorders. It aims to help people change both their avoidance behaviours and the negative thought patterns that drive their anxiety, and sufferers are also usually encouraged to do daily relaxation and to do some exercise, if possible.

ANXIETY DISORDERS AND MINDFULNESS

Relaxation can be quite a challenge for a person whose anxiety is out of control, and some people find that it's easier to make a commitment to mindful meditation. You can start by accepting your anxiety and your thoughts, without trying to change them, and this may be less difficult in the early stages of recovery.

By meditating on a daily basis, you can gradually learn to disengage from your thoughts and the internal dialogue that you have with yourself. Gradually, the thoughts will lose their power and the hold they have over you, and return to their proper place in your life – as just thoughts.

Panic attacks

For many people, their anxiety disorder starts with a panic attack. This enormous surge of physical sensations is terrifying and overwhelming. It is actually a huge fight or flight response that appears to come from nowhere, although discussion with a therapist will usually show that there were warning signs of bad stress that the person ignored or thought they could cope with. A panic attack is usually short-lived, but leaves an indelible terror of having another one. This terror is the driving force behind the associated anxiety disorder.

Most people's response to a panic attack is to quickly leave wherever they happen to be (the flight part of fight or flight), and very often they find that they never want to return to that place again, in case they have another panic attack there. It can be difficult to accept that the attack doesn't stop because you get up and leave; it stops because it was always going to be short-lived. In other words, it was always going to stop, and would have stopped even if you had stayed put. You also feel a little better when you're moving, since the fight or flight response is designed to give you physical energy and simply moving about will burn off some of that energy and make you feel more comfortable.

Traditional therapies have tried to find various ways of encouraging a person to face and sit out a panic attack. It's quite true that, if you can do this, the surge of panic will quite quickly reach a peak and then wash over you and subside. It is, however, extremely difficult to do, and many people find it quite impossible.

PANIC AND MINDFULNESS
Mindfulness practice will teach you to observe your emotions without engaging with them. Remember the value of repetition – by meditating every day, you will build up your ability to sit quietly and observe your anxious feelings. There is a technique known as 'reframing', which means that you learn to change your attitude to your fearful thoughts. You notice and accept them, but you don't engage with them.

Loving-kindness meditation will help you feel more kindly towards your panicky thoughts. They are trying to protect you from threat, after all, which is a good thing, even though in your rational mind you know that there is no real threat. You can learn to be grateful for this attempt to protect you while at the same time accepting that the threat is imaginary.

Obsessive-compulsive disorder (OCD)

People with OCD have obsessive thoughts, which they try to cancel out by carrying out ritualistic compulsions, such as hand washing a certain number of times or counting lampposts in a certain way. Some compulsions are mental, such as doing sums or saying a prayer. The obsessive thoughts can be about a wide range of things, from a fear of germs to the safety of loved ones.

The thoughts are what drive the OCD. They have a strong hold and can seem impossible to resist, and carrying out the compulsions can seem like the only way of getting any peace from them. It doesn't work, of course. Mindfulness can help you first accept that they are there and then go on to gently disengage from them.

OCD AND MINDFULNESS

One technique, known as response delay, is designed to gradually increase the amount of time between the obsessive thought (such as 'I must wash my hands because of the germs') and the actual action (washing your hands). Mindfulness can help you get through this time (even a few seconds can feel far too long to wait). Use a three-minute breathing space for this – it can be much shorter than three minutes, of course.

Jeffrey Schwartz of the UCLA School of Medicine realized that the principles of mindfulness could be used to help people with OCD. His programme covers four main steps, which he calls Relabel, Reattribute, Refocus and Revalue. In essence, the idea is to create a space between your thoughts and your behaviours, and to reduce the power of your thoughts to control you. Schwartz has used brain scans to show that it is possible to change how your brain works by changing your behaviour, something that offers great hope for OCD sufferers.

Focus points

1 Normal anxiety is helpful.
2 Anxiety is part of the fight or flight response.
3 Long-term anxiety can become permanent.
4 Anxiety feels too uncomfortable to tolerate.
5 Meditation can reduce background anxiety.
6 Anxiety disorders are driven by thoughts.
7 Use mindful techniques to disengage from the thoughts.
8 Panic attacks are overwhelming.
9 Use loving kindness to help you accept panic.
10 OCD starts with obsessive thoughts.

Next step

The next chapter is about how a mindful approach can help with sadness and depression.

25

A mindful approach to sadness

In this chapter you will learn:

- ▶ *about sadness and low mood*
- ▶ *about depression and depressive illness*
- ▶ *about mindfulness-based cognitive therapy.*

Sadness and low mood

Sadness is a normal human emotion and we all feel sad from time to time, usually as a result of loss, separation or disappointment. There is some debate over its evolutionary purpose, but it seems likely that it's part of the process of learning from experience – if something makes you sad, you'll put some thought into making sure it doesn't happen again. It's also true that when you're noticeably sad you're more likely to get help and support from other people, which might have been crucial to our survival in the past.

For some of us it is particularly difficult to face and experience sadness. It doesn't produce the surge of energy that comes with anger, stress or anxiety, and as a result there isn't much for Doing mode to grab on to. Crying can bring some relief, but we can be left with the feeling that there's no way of letting sadness out; there's only avoidance and distraction.

You may also feel something along the lines of 'If I let myself start crying, I may never stop.' If that's the case, begin by allowing yourself to face that fear. Is it rational? Is it really likely that the tears will never stop? Are you doing yourself more harm by holding them in than by letting them out? As we know, emotions are short-lived and sadness is no different. Tears can be cathartic and cleansing.

Here are some mindful ways of facing sadness:

▶ If you feel sad when you meditate, acknowledge this and accept it. Don't try to push it away – remember that we all have negative feelings at some point.

▶ If you're aware of the cause of your sadness, acknowledge and accept that, too. Whether your sadness comes from an event outside your control or something that you could have done differently, accept that you can't change the past.

▶ Allow yourself to feel your sadness and be ready to move on when the time is right.

Try it now: Accept your low mood

If you're experiencing low mood, it's important to continue with your regular daily practice. During meditation, allow yourself to observe any sadness that appears. Identify where you feel it physically and imagine yourself breathing into the sadness. Try not to engage in an internal dialogue, rewriting the past or explaining the sadness away. Allow it to just be, and treat yourself gently while you're feeling sad.

Key idea

All emotions – even those of sadness – pass eventually.

Depression and depressive illness

If your sadness becomes chronic and long-term, then you may have an illness known as clinical depression. It seems that depression often strikes people who have an ingrained habit of avoiding emotions.

Self-assessment: Might I be depressed?

How many of these statements do you agree with? Answer with a yes or no, but only answer yes if you feel like this most of the time and have done so for at least two weeks.

1 I feel depressed most of the time.

2 I'm always tired and have no energy.

3 I keep feeling guilty.

4 There's no fun any more.

5 I can't seem to concentrate.

6 I eat too much.

Depression is an illness and, however hard you try, you can't just snap out of it. Nevertheless, there are things you can do to help yourself, especially if your depression is comparatively mild, such as:

► take exercise

► talk through your feelings

► join a self-help group

► eat well

► turn to the people who care about you

► keep doing the things you enjoy (or used to enjoy)

► get out into the fresh air

► listen to music

► watch, read or listen to comedy

► spend time with a pet animal.

If finding the motivation for recovery work is difficult, remember that it's OK to start with very small steps. It's also true that you don't need to believe that these things will work for you, or even be fully engaged with them. Just by doing them, you will start the process of change (remember – repetition changes the brain).

MINDFULNESS AND DEPRESSION

Regular mindful meditation will help you accept and detach from the emotions that are feeding your depression instead of avoiding them or blanking them out. If you have already established a routine for meditation, it will stand you in good stead if later on you become depressed. If you decide to explore mindfulness for the first time during a bout of depression, then do check with your doctor first, and do be gentle with yourself.

Mindfulness is not a quick fix, but by starting with small steps you may be able to find moments of peace while you meditate. A body scan will help you locate where you carry your sad feelings, and you may be able to breathe into them, which can be soothing. Use a three-minute breathing space if you feel yourself slipping into rumination, which can be a feature of depression.

Remember this

Don't try to self-diagnose depression – talk to your doctor.

RECURRING DEPRESSION

For some people, depression can recur. This may be because, between the bouts of depression, they continue with their habit of avoiding their emotions. It's understandable, too – if a lifetime of avoidance was a factor in depression to start with, then the actual experience of depression will make you even more likely to want to avoid unpleasantness. But if you treat every passing negative emotion as a sign that the depression is coming back, then you'll actually be feeding a deep reservoir of avoided emotions.

Another factor seems to be negative thinking and rumination. If you're constantly blaming yourself, feeling useless, judging your life to be a failure and so on, then you'll be creating the perfect atmosphere for depression to breed.

When you meditate, try to observe these negative thoughts but don't engage with them. Try not to judge yourself. Buddhists believe that, although we are all unhappy a lot of the time, we do all yearn to be happy. You do, too, and you haven't deliberately made yourself sad. Treat it mindfully, as something that will pass.

Mindfulness-based cognitive therapy (MBCT)

Following the success of MBSR (see Chapter 22), a new therapy was developed for people with depression. It combines mindfulness with cognitive behaviour therapy (CBT) and so it's known as mindfulness-based cognitive therapy. It has the same eight-week structure and group setting as MBSR, with many of the same exercises, but the focus is on learning about your emotions and how the way you process them can contribute to depression.

The CBT aspect looks at the damage done by avoiding emotions, and shows you how to challenge negative thoughts, and also looks at the effect of rumination.

In the UK, MBCT is recommended by the National Institute of Clinical Excellence (NICE) for people who have had three or more episodes of clinical depression, so, if that is the case for you, ask your doctor to refer you to an MBCT group. You actually attend the group when you are feeling well, since the aim of it is to prevent a relapse.

Focus points

1 Sadness is a normal emotion.
2 Sometimes sadness arises during meditation.
3 In Doing mode, sadness is hard to accept.
4 Sadness can tip over into depression.
5 Exercise, music, fresh air and comedy all help with depression.
6 Being with people, talking and pets all help with depression.
7 Meditation helps you face and accept emotions.
8 Depression can recur.
9 No one chooses to be depressed.
10 MBCT is available free on the NHS.

Next step

The next chapter discusses how mindfulness and meditation can help with many physical health problems.

26

Mindfulness and physical health

In this chapter you will learn:

- ▶ *about the mind–body connection*
- ▶ *mindful strategies for health and healing*
- ▶ *about overcoming tiredness and raising energy levels*
- ▶ *how to ease pain and other discomforts.*

Remember this

If you have a chronic or severe health problem, talk to your doctor before starting mindfulness practice.

Research has shown that meditation is directly helpful with some physical health problems such as high blood pressure, bronchial asthma and tension headaches. Clearly, if your physical illness is stress related and you take steps to reduce your stress, then you're likely to see some improvement – this includes illnesses such as psoriasis and chronic fatigue syndrome. The stress hormone cortisol seems to be implicated in various illnesses, and stress also seems to have a negative impact on your immune system, so again if you reduce your stress you're likely to see an improvement in your immune system and your physical health.

And, of course, illness is stressful in itself, whatever its cause, so anything that helps you cope with and reduce bad stress will also help you cope with ill health. Chronic physical illness can lead to you becoming depressed, so anything that helps you with depression will be of benefit. Mindfulness scores on so many counts.

The mind–body connection

We are only just beginning to understand in a scientific way what many ancient belief systems have always told us – that the mind and the body are interlinked. Your mental attitude can have a huge impact on your physical sense of well-being – or ill-being. This is particularly important if you're facing an illness that is likely to go on for a long time or that will always be with you.

You may find it hard to accept that your mental attitude can have much impact on your physical state, and yet you know that happiness (mental) makes you smile (physical) and sadness (mental) makes you cry (physical). You also know that pain (physical) can make you miserable (mental) and so on. Consider this scenario:

You come home from work feeling worn out, too tired to cook or do anything. In fact, you think you might be going down with a cold. You curl up on the sofa with a hot drink – then the doorbell goes. Not only is it someone you're very fond of, but they're clutching your favourite takeaway. Suddenly, you forget the cold and the tiredness, open a bottle of wine and have a great evening.

We've all experienced something similar to this, just as we've all noticed how children can feel too ill to go to school but quite well enough to play with their favourite toys.

Mindful strategies for health and healing

If you're already living with a chronic health problem, then starting a mindfulness programme will still produce benefits. It may be difficult to find the motivation to do this, so start small and take your time. Try to look on mindfulness as a welcome distraction from the tedious business of being ill, and allow yourself to explore it a little more each day. Don't, however, think of it as a quick fix and don't pin your hopes on a sudden miraculous change. Accept that it's a slow, organic process.

Here's what to include in a mindfulness programme for health and healing:

▶ **Daily meditation**
  Meditate daily, and build up a practice that will stand you in good stead if you become ill. As you progress, you'll become increasingly aware of your inner being, the piece of you that isn't your thoughts, or your emotions, but is just you, and that stays being you whatever your state of physical health.

▶ **Mindful breathing and mini meditations**
  Mindful breathing gives you a way of acknowledging any tension you may be carrying, perhaps because of pain, or around the area of recent treatment. If you have symptoms that come and go, try using mini meditations to help you cope with the bad times.

► **Body scans**
Regular body scans will keep you in tune with your body and make you more responsive to your physical needs. As you breathe into areas of tension, you'll be able to explore the tension and you may find that it dissolves away. Don't aim for this, as your body may not be ready for it, but let it happen when the time is right.

► **Loving-kindness meditation**
Loving-kindness meditation will help you nurture yourself and pay attention to your own needs. It's common now for people to be discharged from hospital at the earliest opportunity, and it's true that for most of us home is the best place to be. However, we can easily slip into ignoring the need to convalesce and try to get back to normal life too quickly. Loving-kindness meditation will remind you of the need to care for yourself while you recover.

Key idea

Mindful detachment gives you a way of separating yourself out from your illness. Just like thoughts and emotions, your illness isn't you. You can also learn not to judge yourself, and not to engage with thoughts such as 'I'm damaged'. Instead, you can acknowledge that the illness is there and you can accept that there may be good days and bad days.

Understanding tiredness

Feeling tired seems to be endemic in our society. It can be a symptom of physical illness, it can be a mental problem, it can mean you're perfectly well but you're doing too much, or it can even mean that you're perfectly well but you're doing too little.

If you're excessively tired, it's always worth talking to your doctor about it – you may have something as simple as a poor diet leading to an iron deficiency. Whether you find out that there is no physical reason for your tiredness, or that feeling tired turns out to be part of a larger health problem, you can set about assessing and dealing with it.

Self-assessment: Understand your tiredness

Try to assess when you become tired, and whether there is a reason for it. This questionnaire will help you consider the possible causes of your tiredness.

1 Are you tired the day after a poor night's sleep, or perhaps a couple of days later?

2 Are you tired after travelling?

3 Are you more tired on Friday than on Monday?

4 Are you more tired if you skip breakfast?

5 Are you more tired if you're too busy to eat?

6 Are you tired if you forget to drink enough?

7 Are you tired after eating certain foods, e.g. dairy products?

8 Are you tired after a heavy meal?

9 Are you more tired when you're worried about something?

10 Do certain kinds of weather affect your energy levels?

11 What is the natural ebb and flow of your energy levels?

Use your journal to record your energy levels for a couple of weeks, using the questionnaire as a guide. You may well start to see a pattern.

Whatever is going on for you, the journal will help you see things more clearly. Some problems will be easy to correct, for instance if you're tired when you skip breakfast, then get up a little earlier and eat something. It doesn't have to be the full cooked breakfast – save that for a special treat – have cereal, wholemeal toast or yoghurt and fruit. Dehydration is a very common cause of tiredness and is easily remedied by drinking more water.

Regular exercise actually lifts energy levels rather than depleting them. Exercise mindfully, in the fresh air if possible, and reap a double benefit by being fully in the present moment.

A lot of tiredness is actually driven by mental activity. Running round busily on autopilot, while all the time thinking of a thousand and one things that need doing, should have been done, will never get done and so on is quite exhausting. Remind yourself to come out of autopilot and connect mindfully with the task in hand. It's far less tiring to focus on one thing at a time.

Use a body scan to connect with your physical tiredness – you may find that you're able to soothe it away, or that you can relax into a short refreshing sleep. If you aren't in a suitable place for napping like this, then use a three-minute breathing space to clear your mind and refresh yourself.

As part of your regular practice, you can use the meditation for energy in Chapter 15, and you can also try short, mini meditations focusing on energy.

Try it now: Do a mini meditation for energy

Start with mindful breathing. Focus on your breathing, and if your mind wanders, gently bring it back. Once your mind is settled, keep your focus on your breathing, but when you breathe in be very aware that you are taking in energy-giving oxygen. Feel it enter your body and move to your centre, just under your ribcage. As you breathe out, feel that energy move outwards through your body. With each breath it moves a little further.

When your whole body is energized, return to mindful breathing. When you end the meditation, take a few moments to return to your everyday life, and then carry on, full of energy.

Pain and other discomforts

Physical pain is there for a reason – it warns us that there is damage to the body, and that we need to see to it. Years ago, I knew a man who didn't feel pain. I quickly learned not to be envious of this. He had to be so careful to monitor his body in other ways. In fact, when he had acute appendicitis, he found out only because his wife noticed his terrible pallor and called the doctor.

To do its job, pain has to be unpleasant – which is why, of course, we are so keen to avoid it. However, when we have an illness that causes chronic, long-term pain, perhaps a different strategy is called for.

The way we deal with pain is often with the second arrow of suffering. You can't ignore pain, but you can add to your physical pain by reacting to it with mental agony. Pain can make us angry, resentful or depressed, but whether we give up or fight back, the pain is still there. It's interesting that mindfulness, which asks you to face and fully experience your pain, can often lead to a reduction in pain. In other words, when you allow yourself to experience it fully, you see its exact size and it may turn out to be smaller than you thought.

Try it now: Do a meditation to ease pain

Choose a meditation posture that is comfortable for you, or that is the least uncomfortable.

Take a few moments to breathe mindfully, feeling your breath. If you find that the pain distracts you, accept this but gently bring your mind back to your breathing.

When you're settled, deliberately take your awareness to the pain. Breathe into the pain, and out of the pain. Take your awareness to the areas around the pain. Breathe into those areas, and out. We create a lot of extra pain by holding the body awkwardly, which creates painful tension and stiffness in the surrounding muscles. Breathing like this may be able to ease and soothe some of the pain.

Focus points

1 Mental attitude has an impact on physical health.
2 Meditation practice helps you cope with illness.
3 Mindful breathing helps release physical tensions.
4 A body scan makes you more sensitive to your body.
5 Your illness isn't you.
6 Tiredness can become chronic.
7 On autopilot, you can forget to monitor your energy levels.
8 You can meditate for energy.
9 Pain has a purpose.
10 Accepting pain often diminishes it.

Next step

The next chapter explains how we often eat for emotional rather than physical reasons, and how mindful eating can make us more aware of our true dietary needs.

Mindfulness and diet

In this chapter you will learn:

▶ *about emotional eating*
▶ *how to assess your eating habits*
▶ *about the benefits of mindful eating*
▶ *how mindfulness can help break the pattern of eating disorders.*

Emotional eating

We all know more or less what it takes to eat healthily, but very few of us manage it. We know that we need to eat enough food for our needs – enough to provide energy for whatever our level of physical activity, and enough nutrition for our bodily functions. However, we don't just eat for these physical reasons, we also eat for emotional reasons. We often eat when we are bored, angry, emotionally empty, feeling stressed or having cravings (e.g. for sugar). This is comfort eating.

The problem with comfort eating is that the comfortable feeling soon wears off. Eating may provide a quick fix, a knee-jerk reaction to an uncomfortable feeling, but, like all avoidance behaviours, it creates a net curtain between our emotions and ourselves.

We also frequently eat on autopilot, while walking along the street, answering emails, watching television, listening to the radio or reading a magazine. Your hand keeps putting food in your mouth, but your mind is elsewhere. For example, I remember eating in front of the television and becoming aware that my dog was watching me. His eyes never left my hand, tracking it from the plate to my mouth and back again. He was totally focused on me and my food – much more than I was.

On the other hand, there are some people whose reaction to stress, anxiety or depression is to lose all appetite. They can feel as if their throat has closed up, that they can't swallow, or that the plateful of food repulses them. They take no comfort in eating, but their behaviour is potentially just as damaging to their bodies as comfort eating.

Whether we overeat or under-eat, it shows a lack of respect for the food, which we are after all very lucky to have. Plenty of people don't have enough to eat, and most of us work hard to get the money to pay for our food.

Many of us also tend to eat very quickly and this doesn't give the brain time to register a feeling of fullness. Research suggests that it takes between 10 and 20 minutes for the brain to register that your stomach is full. We're used to much quicker reactions, for instance if you hit your thumb with a hammer it doesn't take your brain 20 minutes to go 'Ouch!' This means that we aren't always consciously aware of the delay and we keep on eating long after we've had enough.

Case study

Lesley always had three biscuits at tea break; she felt she needed them. Then one day she was called out urgently halfway through her break, so she just grabbed her car keys and ran. Not only did she have only two biscuits, but some minutes later she realized that she felt perfectly full enough. She had been eating the third biscuit before her brain had had a chance to register the first two.

Self-assessment: Understand your eating habits

Try to assess your eating habits, and work out whether you comfort eat or under-eat.

1 Do you eat more when you're stressed?

2 Do you eat less when you're stressed?

3 Do you skip breakfast on working days when you're rushed?

4 Do you snack on autopilot in front of the television?

5 Do you eat in secret?

6 Do you avoid meals and fill up on snacks?

7 Do you crave sugar when you're tired?

8 Do you forget to eat when you're busy?

For a couple of weeks, keep a food diary. Record everything you eat, the time of day, what you were doing and how you were feeling. You'll be able to see the pattern of your eating habits.

The journal will help you begin to understand the emotional side of your eating habits. You may find that there is nothing you need to address, that you eat just enough calories for your physical needs and that you don't use food as a way of soothing yourself. However, if you do comfort eat, being aware of your behaviour and accepting it is the first step to making changes.

You may realize that you are eating as a way of escaping from or avoiding unpleasant emotions. It's important to understand that, however much you enjoy food, eating will never actually be effective as a way of dealing with emotions. Like all unhealthy avoidance behaviours, the effect will quickly wear off and you'll be left with exactly the same problems as you had before.

The dieting culture

Many of us are always on one sort of diet or another. We're encouraged to lose weight in pursuit of an unrealistic body based on airbrushed celebrity photos, or to gain weight in all the right places to get bigger breasts or manly muscles. Whether we're trying to gain or lose weight, dieting makes us obsessed with food. A restrictive diet makes us yearn for the foods we can't have, possibly leading to binge eating when we fall off the wagon. The dieting culture leads us to hate the body we have, to aim for a different body and to reach for unattainable goals. Dieting creates a 'second arrow of suffering', big time.

The mindful approach to diet

Your regular mindfulness practice will create a basic awareness of your body and its needs. You'll also start to be aware of the space between a thought or feeling and your reaction to it. As your awareness increases, the space will seem bigger, and you'll be more able to respond mindfully rather than react mindlessly. So whether you're someone who reaches for the chocolate when the stress builds up, or can't face lunch during a stressful day, you'll become more aware of what you're doing and why. This is the first step towards making changes, and you'll be able to direct your mindful awareness on to your eating habits, using the insight gained from your food journal.

The mindful eating exercises in Part one were part of the process of learning to be fully in the present, and clearly, if you eat slowly and with no distractions, you will feel far more satisfied at the end of the meal.

Cooking and eating mindfully

We are, perhaps, too inclined to let other people do the cooking. When you buy a ready-meal or a takeaway, you see only the finished product and are quite unaware of the processes that produced the food. We all say that the kitchen is the heart of the home, and yet we're often reluctant to spend time there. So try cooking for yourself regularly. Instead of rushing to throw a snack together, take your time and enjoy the process. Anything you've cooked yourself will mean more to you, and you'll be more likely to savour it when you eat it. One reason I enjoy my cake so much is that it's usually homemade, since I regularly get together with friends and we take it in turns to make the cakes.

If you tend to overeat, then cooking for yourself will help you with portion control, and you'll know exactly how much fat, salt and sugar is in the food. If you tend to eat too little, then you can cook things that you know you like, done to your taste, and served in small portions if that's what you prefer – just try to have several a day.

Once you've finished cooking, take a moment to be mindfully aware that you are about to eat. The old habit of saying grace before a meal was a valuable one, and whatever your beliefs it is a good idea to have a small pause before eating anything, in which you acknowledge how lucky you are to have food, and prepare yourself for the pleasure of eating it.

Try it now: Eat a meal mindfully

Before you sit down to your mindful meal, make sure that there are no distractions. Turn off the computer, television, radio and phone. Put away any newspapers, books and magazines. Decide to eat sitting up at the table, not slouched on the sofa with a tray.

1. Serve the food, and take a few moments of mindful breathing.
2. Turn your awareness to the food in front of you. Close your eyes, and smell it. Then look at it, taking in everything about it. Remember to be grateful that you have enough to eat.
3. Next, check your body sensations. Do you feel hungry? Are there any emotions or thoughts?
4. Take the first mouthful of food, and put down your knife, fork or spoon while you chew. Feel the food in your mouth, its temperature, taste and texture. Chew it well before you swallow, and when you swallow, be aware of how it feels.
5. Be aware of your empty mouth before picking up the cutlery to take another mouthful, and eat that in the same way.
6. As the meal progresses, become aware of a feeling of fullness in your stomach. When you are full, stop eating.

Self-assessment

How did that feel? If you overeat habitually, then eating slowly and mindfully will seem very strange. If you under-eat, you may well be used to eating slowly, reluctantly taking each forkful. However, mindfulness asks you to fully engage with the taste and texture of the food rather than choking it down because you know you must.

By taking the following actions, you will gradually reprogramme your eating habits:

▶ Try to eat mindfully at least once a day. Make it a part of your practice, a time for you when you just eat and forget about emails, to-do lists and the tyranny of the clock.

▶ If you have more than one course at a meal, take a short break between them.

▶ Remember to be kind to yourself. Unhealthy eating habits are often about low self-esteem, so when you meditate remember to accept yourself as you are.

▶ Accept that there will be slip-ups, days when you eat a whole box of chocolates on autopilot, or days when you forget to eat because you're so busy. Accept this and forgive yourself.

Eating disorders

Eating disorders cover a wide range – anorexia and bulimia nervosa and binge eating are the most widely known. Anyone with an eating disorder requires medical help, but mindfulness can be usefully incorporated into a recovery programme. If you have obsessive thought patterns about food, then meditation will help you accept and detach from them. If, as is often the case, you are using eating or not eating as a way of blanking out emotions, then mindfulness will help you both accept this and then move to a point where you can start to let the emotions emerge. A regular body scan will put you back in touch with your body and its true needs. Above all, loving-kindness meditations, focusing on yourself, will nurture you and help build up your self-esteem.

Mindfulness-based eating awareness training (MB-EAT)

Mindfulness-based eating awareness training was developed in the United States by Dr Jean Kristeller and colleagues, using the model of MBSR (see Chapter 22) and including aspects of CBT. As you might expect, it is a programme of formal sessions aimed at helping people achieve a mindful perspective on food and eating. You learn to pay attention to your body and to observe your thoughts and emotions, whether positive or negative. There are few courses in the UK at the time of writing, but this is changing.

Focus points

1 We eat for emotional as well as physical reasons.
2 The comfort of eating wears off.
3 Some people can't eat when stressed.
4 Check whether you comfort eat.
5 Dieting often has unrealistic goals.
6 The diet culture creates unrealistic body images.
7 If you cook your own food, it means more.
8 Take your time when you eat.
9 Accept that some days you will revert to bad eating habits.
10 Mindfulness can be part of recovery from eating disorders.

Next step

The next chapter has more on relationships, and explains how to use mindfulness to enhance work and personal relationships including those with your partner and children.

28

More on relationships

In this chapter you will learn:

▶ *about mindfulness at work and mindful work relationships*
▶ *about mindful personal relationships*
▶ *about mindful parenting.*

Having a strong and balanced relationship with yourself is the foundation on which all your other relationships are built. If you bring unresolved issues to your relationships with other people, those issues will always be there, distorting the relationship and causing problems. However, once you are on the road to a mindful relationship with yourself, you can start to look at all the other relationships in your life.

Self-assessment

Make notes in your journal about the various relationships you have with other people – your work colleagues, friends, family members and partner. Decide which are going well and which are problematic.

Mindfulness at work

You can bring a mindful attitude to both the relationship you have with your actual work and the relationships you have with others at work.

THE WORK ITSELF

Whatever your work is, you can do it with mindful awareness. Allow yourself to be fully present in the moment, and aware of the sounds, sights, feel and smells of whatever you are doing. Instead of seeing work as something you have to get through before you can have your real life, try to engage with it fully, however routine and mundane it may seem to you. At the other extreme, if your work is so stressful that you often feel unable to disengage when you're not at work, then mindfulness will help you turn off the autopilot and detach yourself from the stress.

Try it now: Be mindful at work

1 Choose a time to be mindful at work. Try to be fully present and engaged with your work for at least an hour.
2 Try a three-minute breathing space at the end of your day's work, either during the commute (not if you're driving, though) or as soon as you get home. It's important to leave work behind at the appropriate time.

YOUR WORKING RELATIONSHIPS

Working relationships are usually less emotional than your personal relationships, but equally they can become very frustrating. You didn't choose the person at the next desk or bench to you, and yet you have to find a way to get along with them.

Very often, the simple act of mindful listening will keep things (or put them back) on track. In a busy work environment, it's easy to forget to pay attention to people, and yet it's the one thing we all need. If a working relationship still proves difficult, mindfulness will help you disengage from it and keep a sense of perspective. Being mindfully non-judgemental will take some of the heat out of the relationship. If you can't be best buddies, at least you can learn not to engage with the negative.

Finally, don't forget the power of body language. Instead of slumping in your chair, sit up straight, with dignity. This will help your breathing, which in turn will energize you and will also give out a message of calmness and serenity to the people around you, which can only help your relationships.

Mindfulness: singledom and dating

Finding a partner seems to be one of our deepest drives, and being single can feel like a desperate situation. If you feel yourself becoming frantic about the search for a partner, it's time to stand back and take a more mindful attitude. Try observing your feelings and behaviour without judging or trying to change them. Accept that you're currently single. That's how it is. Then bring yourself into the present moment and engage with your life as it is now, letting go of regrets about the past and fantasies about the future.

This will give you a much calmer basis for meeting new people and dating. You can use mindfulness in those situations, too – being fully engaged in the moment rather than fantasizing about your date's potential as a partner or putting energy into creating a false self for public show. Mindfulness practice helps you be comfortable in your own skin, which is a very attractive quality, and you'll also be able to let go of any unrealistic expectations of the other person.

Speed dating is based on the premise that we decide about people within a few seconds of meeting them. Unfortunately, it often degenerates into a frantic attempt to display your entire personality at top speed. Try being mindfully engaged in the moment and focused on the other person; this will give you a far more rewarding experience.

Try it now: Practise mindful dating

The next time you're on a date, use mindfulness to stay anchored in the present. Enjoy the date for what it is, not for what you hope it will be.

Mindfulness: marriage and partnerships

Straight or gay, married or cohabiting, for most of us this is the most important relationship of all. It's certainly the one we want to last the longest – we leave our parents and our children leave us, but we hope that our partner will be there for ever.

This must mean that it's all too easy to live on autopilot, getting into the habit of assuming that you know what the other wants because you've known them for so long. Most relationships start with a period of heady romance, when you are each fully engaged with the other, but this wears off after a while and autopilot takes over. It's important to make time to come out of autopilot and be fully in the present when you're with your partner, however long you've been together.

In autopilot mode we also tend to have knee-jerk reactions, which can become entrenched habits. The more you meditate, the more you'll be able to detach and observe yourself, and this insight will show you how you bring your own needs to the relationship – we ask more of our significant other than any other relationship in life. If you expect them to meet all your needs, they may buckle under the weight. Instead, look at how far you can look after yourself, and allow your relationship to be nurturing but not needy.

One very common need is the craving to be understood. Do you feel that if someone truly loves you they will always understand you? Experience shows us that this is an unrealistic expectation, and yet it is very hard to let go of it. Even after many years together, you won't know everything there is to know about someone, and you'll never fully understand them. If you can accept this, and accept that no relationship is perfect, then you'll have far more chance of being happy and content.

Try it now: Focus on your partner

Make a specific commitment to spend time with your partner in a mindful way. Identify the times and activities that make you feel most securely connected with them and choose one of those. Then find out what makes them feel connected with you, and make time for that as well.

Mindfulness-based relationship enhancement (MBRE)

Mindfulness-based relationship enhancement is a relatively recent development based on MBSR (see Chapter 22). It aims to help couples to enrich and improve their relationship. It starts, of course, with meditation practice but there is an emphasis on open communication and mindful listening. It is not marriage guidance; rather it is for couples who are relatively happy and not feeling distress in the relationship, but who would like to become even closer and more empathic with each other.

Mindfulness and divorce

Mindful practice in relationships is not about keeping them going whatever the cost. Sometimes relationships reach their natural end. Sometimes divorce and break-ups are inevitable.

This is a huge loss, and it can help to recognize this and treat it as a bereavement (see Chapter 29). Take time to nurture and soothe yourself, and use your regular mindful meditation sessions to create a space where you can just Be. There are so many painful emotions such as anger, resentment, grief and betrayal to deal with that a degree of avoidance is probably inevitable, but if you're aware of this you can gradually face and accept each one. Because the emotional impact is so complicated, you will also inevitably find yourself facing the 'second arrow of suffering' (see Chapter 14), but again, by being aware of this, you can detach from it and try to let it go.

When you feel so much pain, it's easy to want the other person to suffer too, and yet deep down you probably know that this won't make you feel any better. Loving-kindness meditation extended to the other person may seem a lot to ask, but start in the usual way with kindness to yourself, and non-judging, and see where that leads you.

Mindful parenting

We've already seen that children live fully in the present, but without being able to detach themselves from their emotions. As parents and caregivers, we are able to help them with that, but we often forget to help ourselves at the same time.

BABIES

A small baby is programmed to cry to express its needs, and we are programmed to respond. This makes us very solution-focused when a baby cries, and it's important that we think through the basics such as hunger, thirst and a dirty nappy, then move on to more worrying possibilities such as pain and illness. But on the days when a baby just cries and there seems to be no solution, mindful acceptance will help you through those times. In fact, it will have a practical impact too, since a fretful baby is more likely to be soothed if the person holding it is calm, with peaceful breathing and a steady heartbeat.

TODDLERS

A toddler can seem like a ticking bomb – at any minute he or she might explode into a tantrum of frustration or aggression, added to which they have an insatiable curiosity and no sense of danger. Finding the time to meditate can seem impossible, since you can never leave a toddler unattended, and the rare moments when they are asleep or at nursery are used for catching up with your life and, inevitably, your sleep.

If you regard your meditation practice as an fundamental part of your well-being – an essential part of your body maintenance rather like cleaning your teeth – then you are more likely to find the time for it. And it will be worth while. Instead of feeling that the toddler stage will never end, you're more likely to be able to see it as a short phase in your child's journey through life. Your empathy with their frustrations will increase, and so will your ability to stay calm and use distraction rather than shouting.

You'll also be able to look at your own behaviour and ask yourself whether perhaps your expectations are too high. If you have little experience of small children, it may come as a shock to realize how short their attention span is, how poor their memory, how lacking their impulse control. In other words, you'll have to remind them constantly with endless repetitions and reminders of how you need them to behave.

On difficult days, make full use of the three-minute breathing space – even a 30-second breathing space will ground you and give you back a sense of perspective. However obstinate your toddler may seem, they do in fact tend to mirror their parents' behaviour, so that the more you can be calm, empathic, and warm, the more likely they are to copy you.

OLDER CHILDREN

As children become older and have better verbal skills, it becomes easier to communicate and explain things to them. They bring more and more to the relationship as their personalities develop, and you are constantly adjusting to the changes. Regular mindfulness practice will help you achieve ongoing insight so that you adapt in real time rather than lagging behind, clinging on to the child that used to be instead of acknowledging the child that is.

You'll also be able to notice any bad habits you're reproducing from your own childhood. Of course, we all resolve not to copy our own parents' faults and to mimic their good points, but some negative ways can still creep in unnoticed.

In our very busy lives, it can be easy to forget the concept of quality time or perhaps to have too little of it. The one thing that all children need is plenty of attention, and naughtiness can be simply a way of getting what they need – even punishment is better than being ignored.

Try it now: Take time out from parenting

When your children are driving you to distraction, take a three-minute breathing space as a time out for yourself. Give yourself what you need, and then move on to considering what it is that they need.

One common difficulty is to have over-high expectations, either because you can see your child's potential or because you want them to make the most of the opportunities you never had. My son's piano teacher told me that if he practised more he had the potential to be a professional musician. My son stubbornly insisted that he wanted to play football instead of practise. After much discussion, he actually gave up music for a while, only to return to it later with renewed passion. He'll never be a professional musician – but he is happy.

It can be very hard to accept that your children are beginning to make their own decisions, and to accept that while they may, like my son, have a certain amount of talent, they may not have the desire or drive to pursue it. Equally, they may be interested in something you see as pointless or unlikely to lead to the kind of life you want for them. Mindful detachment will help you see that these feelings are about you, not about your child.

Try it now: Listen mindfully to your child

If you have to talk to a child about their reluctance to do something, or about interests that you find unsuitable, try to let go of your agenda and give your full mindful attention to what the child is saying.

Finally, all parents need to remember that they haven't got their children for very long and sometimes they should just enjoy them. Remember to be playful, light-hearted and joyful with your children.

Try it now: Play with your child

Make time every day to do something pointless and silly with your child or children.

Focus points

1 Use mindful listening at work.
2 Let go of expectations on dates.
3 Long-term relationships can slip into autopilot.
4 Take care of your own needs.
5 Use mindfulness during relationship break-ups.
6 Children copy their parents and carers.
7 Use three-minute breathing spaces when children are being difficult.
8 Give mindful attention to children.
9 Accept children as they are.
10 Remember to have fun and be silly with your children.

Next step

The next chapter explains how the mindful approach to bereavement can help us cope with the pain of grief.

29

Mindfulness and bereavement

In this chapter you will learn:

▶ *about bereavement and grief*
▶ *about the stages of the grieving process*
▶ *how to use mindfulness to acknowledge and adjust to bereavement.*

Bereavement and grief

The news of death brings us rocketing into full present-moment awareness. Even if we are distant from it, such as when a plane crashes on the other side of the world, it makes us stop and think. Suddenly, everything falls into a clearer perspective and we realize how unimportant most things are compared with the loss of someone we love.

Grief is a normal and natural emotion. It's the other side of the coin from love – if you didn't love and care about other people, then you wouldn't grieve when someone dies. There is a natural cycle of birth and death and your grief is part of that cycle.

When someone we care about dies, the grief we feel can be overwhelming, and the desire to escape from or avoid that pain can also be overwhelming. Like any other emotion, grief will fester if trapped inside you, and if you don't find a way to deal with it you may end up quite unable to function. For some people the intense pain of grief is made worse by the feeling that if they let themselves feel it all, it will somehow be too much, more than they can bear. This is perhaps the sharpest second arrow of suffering of all. The more we struggle not to face the pain, the stronger the pain becomes.

The danger is that such an extreme emotion might trigger extreme avoidance, and that may well be seriously damaging to your well-being. Some people drink too much; others develop depression or anxiety. Most of us lose all sight of caring for ourselves, feeling that nothing matters compared with the pain of our loss.

And yet your life will go on and, as well as grief, you may have to deal with the consequences of the damage done by your avoidance behaviours. Most cultures have mourning rituals, and there is wisdom in this. They create a space in which to work through your grief, while at the same time setting boundaries within which it can be contained.

Key idea

Grief is not a continuous emotion; it waxes and wanes, and changes with time. Various stages of grief have been identified and, although these may vary from person to person, it's clear that grief is a journey rather than a fixed state.

The stages of grief

Various models of grief have been developed over the years. They are no more than guidelines that may help you make sense of what you're going through. You may experience all or only some of the following feelings, and in any order. Everyone is different. You may be:

► numb

► depressed

► angry

► pining

► in denial

► feeling guilty

► feeling abandoned.

In the 1960s Elisabeth Kübler-Ross identified five main stages in facing death (either of oneself or a loved one), which are usually expressed in the following order (although they may be experienced in any order, and not everyone experiences all of them):

1 Denial – 'This can't be happening.'

2 Anger – 'It's not fair.'

3 Bargaining – 'Just a little more time together, please.'

4 Depression – 'Nothing has any point.'

5 Acceptance – 'It comes to all of us sooner or later.'

Bereaved people who have been through some or all of the five stages will have completed part of the grieving process but possibly not all of it. Once they have accepted their loss and experienced the pain of the loss, they still have more work to do. After all, life goes on without the person who has died, and that takes some adjustment. During that process of adjustment, the bereaved person will start to take an interest in their new life and find things that they can engage with. One way of looking at the process of working through grief is to see it as a challenge, perhaps the biggest you will ever face, and each stage of grief will set you a different challenge.

Approaching grief mindfully

In my own experience of bereavement, I found that mindfulness was only one of the many things that helped me: the support of family and friends, the passing of time, counselling and even the need to function in a practical way were all also helpful.

Try to allow yourself to feel whatever you need to feel at that moment in time. Bereavement has many elements, and you can easily start to feel as if you're in a whirlwind, being whisked from one emotion to another. Take a little time each day to allow your emotions to settle and mindfully connect with whichever one is uppermost. Focus on your breathing as a way of staying centred while you allow yourself to feel your emotions. However painful they are, they are part of being human.

Acknowledge that the grief you feel belongs to you, not to the person who has died. Set time aside for a loving-kindness meditation where you can nurture yourself and your terrible feelings of loss. Allow yourself to feel connections with the people who you know care for you.

A body scan will help you locate where in your body you're feeling your emotions, and will also remind you to care for your body's needs. Eat well, and get some fresh air and exercise.

You may find yourself dwelling on missed opportunities – things you wish you'd said or not said, and things you wish you'd done or not done. This is another second arrow of suffering, so allow yourself to let go of it.

Set aside specific times for visiting your grief formally and mindfully, so that at other times you can take care of your everyday needs. You may not feel like keeping to your normal routines, but there can be comfort in quietly doing those things that you've always done.

When you are being mindful, you are creating a distance between yourself and your emotions. You can observe yourself and acknowledge your suffering, but you can also allow yourself to move gently forwards through the grief and, eventually, out the other side.

Focus points

1 News of death resets your sense of perspective.
2 Grief is an aspect of love.
3 The pain of grief can be overwhelming.
4 Reactions to grief can be extreme and damaging.
5 Grief is a journey.
6 There are stages to grief.
7 Eventually there will be a new life after bereavement.
8 Mindfully acknowledge the emotional pain of grief.
9 Stay connected with other people while grieving.
10 Remember to care for yourself while grieving.

Next step

Find out even more about mindfulness through the resources listed in the following section, Taking it further.

Taking it further

Online resources

Free online course http://palousemindfulness.com/ selfguidedMBSR.html – highly recommended.

Mental Health Foundation:
www.mentalhealth.org.uk/
See their report 'Be Mindful', and also their podcasts 'What is Mindfulness?' and '10-Minute Practice Exercise'.

Online course:
www.bemindfulonline.com/

Distance learning:
learnmindfulness.co.uk/mindfulness-courses/ distance-learningmindfulness/

Finding retreats:
www.metta.org.uk/retreats.asp

Mindfulness research:
www.mindfulexperience.org/

Buddhism:
www.thebuddhistsociety.org/

Books

Alidina, S., *Mindfulness for Dummies* (John Wiley & Sons Ltd, 2010)

Carrington, P., *The Book of Meditation* (Anchor Press, 1997)

Crane, R., *Mindfulness-Based Cognitive Therapy* (Routledge, 2009)

Fletcher, E. and Langley, M., *Free Yourself from Anxiety*, (How To Books, 2008)

Gunaratana, B. H., *Mindfulness in Plain English* (Wisdom Publications, 2002)

Heaversedge, J. and Halliwell, E., *The Mindful Manifesto* (Hay House, 2010)

Kabat-Zinn, J., *Full Catastrophe Living: How to Cope with Stress, Pain and Illness Using Mindfulness Meditation* (Piatkus, 1990)

Kabat-Zinn, J., *Wherever You Go, There You Are: Mindfulness Meditation for Everyday Life* (Piatkus, 1994)

Langley, Martha, *The Mindfulness Workbook* (Teach Yourself, 2013)

Schwartz, J. M. with Beyette, B., *Brain Lock: Free Yourself from Obsessive-Compulsive Behavior* (Harper, 1996)

Index